HUMAN EXPERIENCE AND THE ART OF COUNSELLING

HUMAN EXPERIENCE
AND THE
ART OF COUNSELLING

FURTHER CONVERSATIONS

between

A DOCTOR AND A PRIEST

Edited by

MARCUS LEFÉBURE O.P.

T. & T. Clark Ltd

36 George Street, Edinburgh

Copyright © Marcus Lefébure O.P., 1985

Typesetting by Swanston Typesetting, Derby, England
Cover design by Hamish Gordon, Edinburgh, Scotland
Printed and bound by Billing & Sons Ltd., Worcester, England

Printed in England
for
T. & T. CLARK LIMITED
EDINBURGH, SCOTLAND

ISBN: 0 567 29121 9

In memory of my father
and in homage to my mother
with great gratitude to them both
and the hope that what they enabled me to receive
I may be able to pass on to others

Publisher's Note

The predecessor to this book, *Conversations on Counselling*, also featured Dr Martin Gregory as the other partner in the dialogues. Gradually the true identity of the 'doctor' became known and a note declaring it is being inserted in the second, revised edition, published concurrently with this volume. To bring this book into line with the previous one, therefore, we here repeat that Dr Martin Gregory is the pseudonym for Dr Hans Schauder. He is a medical doctor, born in Vienna, educated in Vienna and Basel, and works as an independent counsellor in Edinburgh. He is also associated with the Rudolf Steiner movement and several social work agencies.

acknowledgements

I should like to express my grateful acknowledgement to the following for the use of material quoted in this book: George Allen & Unwin and Harper & Row for quotations from *The Art of Loving* by Erich Fromm (New York, 1956, pp.103-104) and *Outlines of Indian Philosophy* by M. Hiriyanna (London, 1932, pp.18, 20-21, 24); David Bolt Associates Ltd for a quotation from *New Pathways in Psychology: Maslow and the Post-Freudians* by Colin Wilson (London, 1973, pp.22-23); Collins Publishers for a quotation from *Silent Music* by W. Johnston (London, 1974, p.120); Constable Publishers for quotations from *On Becoming a Person* by C. Rogers (London, 1967, pp.17 & 23-24) and *The True Wilderness* by H. Williams (London, 1965, p.12); the executors and the estate of W. Somerset Maugham, William Heinemann Ltd and Doubleday & Co. Inc. for an excerpt from *The Razor's Edge* by W. Somerset Maugham (copyright 1943, 1944 by McCall Corporation, copyright 1944 by W. Somerset Maugham, reprinted by permission of Doubleday & Company Inc., New York, 1944, p.186); Faber & Faber, Publishers for quotations from *The Art of Prayer* by Igumen Chariton of Valamo (London, 1966, p.140) and from *Persons in Relation* by J. Macmurray (London, 1961, pp.17, 61 & 66); Granada Publishing Limited for a quotation from *The Silva Method of Mind Control* by J. Silva and P. Miele (St Albans, Herts, 1980, p.172); William Heinemann Ltd for quotations from *Twentieth Century Mystics and Sages* by A. Bancroft (London, 1976, pp.76 & 157); Verlag Herder GmbH & Co., KG for a passage (in my own translation) from *Wissende, Verschwiegene, Eingeweihte* by H.-J. Baden (Freiburg, 1981, pp.100-101); Hutchinson Publishing Group Ltd for a quotation from *The Way of All Women* by E. Harding (London, 1971, pp.275-276); Insel Verlag for a passage (in my own translation) from *Briefe an einen jungen Dichter* by R. M. Rilke (Leipzig, No. 406, n.d. p.19); Mosaik Verlag for two passages (in my own translation) from *Meditation – Wege zum Selbst* by U. Reiter (Munich, 1976, p.45); Oxford University Press for quotations from *Arthur Schnitzler* by M. Swailes (Oxford, 1971, pp.125-126), *Hinduism* by R. C. Zaehner (Oxford, 1980, pp.125-126, 170-171, 180) and *Natural Law and Natural Rights* by J. Finnis (Oxford, 1980, p.143); Penguin Books for quotations from *Confessions* by St Augustine (Harmondsworth, Middlesex, 1968, pp.211-212) and *Hinduism* by K. M. Sen (Harmondsworth, Middlesex, 1981, pp.13 & 22-23); Prestel Verlag for a passage (in my own translation) from *Die Zauberflöte* by A. Rosenberg (Munich, 1972, p.8); Ernst Reinhardt GmbH & Co Verlag for a passage (in our own translation) from *Der Organismus der Seele* by C. G. Heyer (Munich, 1951, pp.11ff.); Rowohlt Taschenbuch Verlag for a passage (in my own translation) from *Max Reinhardt* by Leonhard M. Fiedler (published in the series 'rowohlts monographien', copyright © 1975 by Rowohlt Taschenbuch Verlag GmbH, Reinbeck bei Hamburg p.38); Search Press for a quotation from *The Dark Night of the Soul* by St John of the Cross (London, 1953, pp.82 & 318); Sheed & Ward for a quotation from *Interior Castle* by Saint Theresa of Avila (London, 1974, p.143); Anthony Sheill Associates Ltd for a quotation from *Travelling In* by Monica Furlong (London, 1971, p.32); Sheldon Press for a quotation from *Conjectures of a Guilty Bystander* by T. Merton (London, 1968, p.158); Rudolf Steiner Press for a quotation from *Knowledge of the Higher Worlds* by R. Steiner (London, 1969, pp.137-138); Rudolf Steiner Nachlassverwaltung for passages (in my own translation) from *Die Welt der Sinne und die Welt des Geistes* by R. Steiner and *Zu Rudolf Steiner's Lebensgang*, Bildband I (Dornoch bei Basel, Switzerland, 1959, pp.32 & 34 and 1971, p.136 respectively); Tavistock Publications for a quotation from *The Divided Self* by R. D. Laing (Pelican Books, Harmondsworth, Middlesex, 1965, p.173); Vendanta Press for quotations from *How to Know God* by Prabhavananada & C. Isherwood (Hollywood, 1966, pp.78-79, 198 & 204). I am also grateful to Mr J. M. Cohen for permission to publish an extract from his translation of *The Life of Saint Teresa* (at p. 210) and to Professor Gerard Rochford for permission to cite a phrase from his inaugural lecture.

I should like to express my gratitude to my confrère, Fr Denis Geraghty, O.P., who assured me that so far as he could see there is nothing 'contrary to faith and morals' in what I say in this book. My quite special thanks, however, are to my brother, Eric, and to Dr Joyce Poole who read through the penultimate draft with meticulous care. Their concern for sense and language helped me to purge at least the more egregious infelicities and howlers.

Marcus Lefébure,
February, 1985.

contents

'We may say ... that the Self exists only in dynamic relation with the Other ...

The original pattern of personal behaviour is not merely a starting-point. It is not left behind as the child grows up. It remains the ground pattern of all personal motivation at every stage of development. If the *terminus a quo* of the personal life is a helpless total dependence on the Other, the *terminus ad quem* is not independence, but a mutual interdependence of equals.'

John Macmurray *Persons in Relation*

'A man truly alive is the glory of God.'

St Irenaeus of Lyons

preface

One reviewer of our previous book *Conversations on Counselling* wittily continued the figure of the dialogue by referring to the book as 'an invitation to eavesdrop' on what he was kind enough to describe as 'a very sensitive exploratory dialogue between a priest and a doctor about very complex ... human relationships and the role of the counsellor in them'. It is in this spirit that I proffer the further dialogues between my friend Dr Martin Gregory and myself collected in this volume. They are therefore a sequel of our previous conversations but they also represent a development of them. On either count they nevertheless have a certain integrity of their own.

In view of the continuity between the two series of conversations, readers of the previous volume may like to be reminded and others may like to be told that the two main conversations were devoted to the dynamic unfolding of the typical counselling relationship as a creative process and to the unfolding of the equally typical stages of spiritual growth. These two dialogues developed into an exploration of two corresponding intuitions: that the counselling process is only an instance, albeit a disciplined and deepened instance, of any truly human encounter as such, and that the phases of the counselling process and stages of spiritual growth could and in principle should interpenetrate each other in an ordered way. These four dialogues were at once punctuated and connected by two further conversations about relationship and solitude, and about the archetypal relationship between woman and man. The dialogue form was meant to express and enact the cooperative and discursive nature of any human search, while the succession of dialogues was meant to suggest its organic character.

As for these conversations being a development of the

1

previous ones, they are so in more ways than one.

They are a development first of all from the point of view of the technique of composition. The basis of both series of dialogues has been real and spontaneous conversations between Dr Gregory and myself. But in our previous volume I sought to keep as close as possible to the tape-recordings of the original conversations. We may as a result have conveyed something of the spontaneity and liveliness of the original meetings, but we may have done so at the price of the loss of a certain economy: the flow was at times not so much sinuous as meandering. Learning from this experience, I decided to exercise my editorial function more vigorously this time. Various consequences followed from this decision.

We continued to meet in Dr Gregory's study, and so he was in a position to reach down the books to which he referred so easily, but I could at the time only give the gist of the quotations from the books in my own room. As a result of the greater freedom I had given myself I was now able to check and incorporate my own references.

More substantially, I was able to rethink and reshape, not only my own responses but the general structure of each conversation. I hope that I have, as a result, achieved a greater spareness of line without losing the sense of immediacy and surprise our conversations seem to have had live. I have thus taken pains to remain as faithful as possible to the exact words of my friend Dr Gregory, and if not to the order of their original utterance, then certainly to the gist of our actual conversations. But much more than in our previous series the original taped conversations relate to the published version more like a quarry to the finished building or sculpture.

One further consequence of this greater liberty has gradually dawned on me in the course of editing this series, and this is the heightened contrast between us. In the original conversations I had contented myself with listening to Dr Gregory and drawing him out, though not without occasional disagreement and counter-argument; but in the recomposition of these dialogues I allowed myself to expand my original thoughts, doing so very much in the style to which my whole training in philosophy and theology had inclined me. As a result what came over in our previous series as a contrast of physical type, experience and formation now comes over much more in terms of a contrast of style and of thinking.

There is a paradox here. I had in the Prologue of the previous volume evoked our respective personalities. Dr Gregory is short, stocky, bald and bright-eyed, now well into his seventies, Jewish in background, medical in training, and every inch the Viennese, whereas I am of medium height, slim, bearded, just into my fifties, born and raised in England, largely trained in law, philosophy and theology, and so, on the surface, an Englishman. But Dr Gregory even in his second language, retains a concreteness of expression that is usually associated with the English genius, whereas I tend to generalise and so have a more abstract style that is more usually associated with the continental mind. He tends to leave the general implications implicit in the image, I want to draw them out. I want to unfold what my friend is happy to leave in seed-form. There are personal and temperamental factors that help to explain this paradox, not least the fact, on my side, for instance, that both my parents were themselves born and brought up in Vienna, my father originally of French nationality on *his* father's side, and the further fact that when I did my studies in Paris, I was particularly impressionable to the Gallic genuis. So although I am myself English by birth and largely by education, I am continental by blood and in large measure also by temperament.

Be that as it may, I am aware that the resulting contrast of styles of reflection could be disconcerting for some readers. I do hope that it will be challenging, even welcome, to others. I also console myself with the thought that in my occasional more speculative elaborations I rarely, if ever, do more than attempt to render in more general and philosophic terms what Dr Gregory says in his more personal way so that readers can, if they so wish, skip over these passages and come back to the earth of my friend's observations! But what I am trying to do in these few instances is to relate his reflections on experience to the general enterprise we call philosophy.

This is the real point. For, as I was working on these dialogues, the conviction again grew in me that philosophy has tended to leave the substance of human experience more or less out of account and so to stray from its original calling as a living 'love of wisdom'. It is true that nature abhors a vacuum so that whenever this has happened there have been corresponding, if more or less unwitting, attempts to fill it. But the double displacement – of philosophy out of the area of real life and of other enterprises into the space thus vacated – has resulted in a mutual loss: philosophy has been emptied of life, but the human projects that have sought to deal with it in its stead have tended to lack that rigour of thinking that has also traditionally been part of philosophy's task. And since psycho-therapy as a discipline of thinking as well as of action is one of the latest and not the least noble of these attempts to fill the vacuum left by philosophy, it too has tended to suffer from the failure to correlate its concepts systematically with each other and with past sets. By expanding somewhat the suggestions I had already made in the live conversations, I was, therefore, trying to do two things simultaneously: to reintegrate some of life's real problems into the general enterprise of philosophy and in the process to contribute to making reflection on life more coherent and complete. My particular effort to tackle this task may be inept and imperfect to a degree, but the attempt to relate philosophy and human experience more intimately to each other surely needs to be made.

A contrast may help elucidate my meaning. I have been speaking of philosophy's calling and its occasional lapses. In so doing, I have been referring to Western philosophy, and the qualification is necessary because philosophy has not fared in the same way in all cultures. The Indian tradition is a case in point. M. Hiriyanna brings this out in a way that is as lucid as it is pertinent. He begins by observing that 'religion and philosophy do not stand sundered in India'. He goes on to say that the distinctive mark of religion is 'that it serves to further right living; and it is only in this sense that we can speak of religion as one with philosophy in India. The ancient Indian did not stop short at the discovery of truth, but strove to realise it in his own experience ... It has been remarked with reference to Jainism that its fundamental maxim is "Do not live to know, but know to live" and that the same may well be said of the other Indian schools also ... philosophy as understood in India is neither mere intellectualism nor mere moralism, but includes and transcends them both. In other words, it aims ... at achieving more than what Logic and Ethics can. But it must not be forgotten that, although not themselves constituting the end, these are the *sole* means of approach to it. They have been represented as the two wings that help the soul in its spiritual flight. The goal that is reached through their aid is characterised on the one hand by jñāna or illumination which is intellectual conviction that has ripened into an immediate experience and, on the other, by vairāgya or self-renunciation which is secure by reason of the discovery of the metaphysical ground for it.'[1] This is excellently put and points to a philosophical approach from which Western philosophy has much to learn. In fact there is scope here for a vast philosophical project which I can only indicate. I want only to alert the reader to the reason why I have been moved to include a few developments which may at first sight appear to be foreign to our main purpose.

This, then, is the reason why I have thought fit to include certain more philosophic elaborations – a concern for the integrity of human experience, the conviction that human experience gains from organised reflection. But the integrity of human experience is also the reason for the second major development to be found in this volume in comparison with the first. It is incidentally, also, above all this development that makes this collection a book on its own.

---

1. *Outlines of Indian Philosophy*, at pp. 18, 20, 24.

I have already referred to the way in which, even on our first series, my friend Dr Gregory had found himself able to articulate what I call, in this book, one of his master-insights, namely, that the *Gespräch*, the dialogue, between counseller and client is only a particular but a crystallised and disciplined version of any truly human communication. It is this perception which has more and more become the principle of this series. We have come to see, with ever greater clarity, that the processes which occur within a counselling relationship are only an intensification of the processes that occur in everyday life, albeit with boundaries other than those of everyday life. The counselling relationship is a variant of any deep and intimate human exchange, but subject to the discipline of some at least implicitly shared purpose; it is a bounded version, a heightened instance of it.

Two things follow from this. On the one hand, it means that counselling may involve certain learnable skills, but that it must, in the end, be grounded in certain basic qualities of concern, common sense and humanity. If I may appropriate the fine phrase Professor Gerard Rochford used in his inaugural lecture at Aberdeen, counselling can be considered to be what he claims social work to be: '*Love's* skilled practice'. On the other hand, it also means that so-called ordinary people may hope to recognise themselves in the more sophisticated descriptions of what goes on in a counselling relationship and so find the daily lives they actually lead enhanced. There is thus a traffic between counselling and life. The lines of flow between them are no doubt numerous, but I have in this book limited consideration to five of them. I reckon that any human being will be gripped by, and welcome the chance to reflect further on, what it is to be creative, the drag of the past and the pull of the future, the play of power in personal relationships, the often conflicting demands of personal growth and a social code, sex and contemplation.

Finally, it is because we have come to see the book more and more in this way that we have by deliberate judgement allowed ourselves to quote other people frequently and at length.

Because what we are concerned with is ultimately not so much the techniques of counselling as the essence of being human revealed in the process, we are glad to acknowledge some of the human spirits who have been our mentors and companions on the way.

It is in this spirit that we offer the following jointly explored reflections on certain aspects or dimensions of counselling. We hope that they will be received as what they are meant to be: meditations on what relationship with another involves – and therefore meditations on human experience.

Dialogue 1:
Counselling and
Creativity

Some four hundred years ago, there lived in India a poet-saint called Rajjab. When it was known that Rajjab had received his 'illumination', men from far and near came to him and asked: 'What is it that you see? What is it that you hear?' He answered: 'I see the eternal play of life. I hear heavenly voices singing, "Give form to the yet unformed, speak out and express."'

Hinduism K.M. Sen[1]

'We've already discussed a great deal together, Martin,' I began this particular morning. 'You'll remember how we first met professionally but soon discovered that we shared so much simply as people, let alone as counsellors. So we began to meet fairly regularly, and our association grew into friendship. In the process we also soon realised that for all our sharing we came to our experiences from our respective starting-points as counsellor and priest as well as from different backgrounds and that this made for a rich contrast and complementarity. So we've already explored our agreement but also raised a number of important issues between us. Inevitably, however, we've left a lot undiscussed. I can glimpse a few of the further topics I should like to talk over with you, and there's one of quite central importance in particular that I'd like to take up with you again. I therefore wonder whether you'd care to start another series of conversations on subjects of mutual concern?'

1. at p.13.

'I should not just care to continue our previous dialogues, Marcus, I should be delighted to do so. These meetings have become very important to me. You're well aware that we've been having these conversations for many years now. When we started, I was already approaching old age, and now I'm experiencing it fully. In these circumstances I have to say that our talks have been a veritable life-line for me. You see, I've always lived on the level of intimate experience which, however, I tried to deepen through a feeling that's possibly akin to artistic feeling. But I'm not naturally articulate. I've never written anything – except a few poems – I've never given a lecture. You, on the other hand, have a gift for thinking, your profession is to speak, and you bring your extensive knowledge of philosophy and theology to bear on anything you discuss. As a result when I'm with you and am – happily! – exposed to your highly trained and searching mind, my thoughts, instead of floating like clouds, begin to condense. I'm very grateful.'

'You're very kind, Martin. I hope you appreciate how even the very contrast of our sensibility nourishes me too. But to our muttons. I've already indicated that the first question I'd like to pursue with you arises out of our previous discussions and it happens to be the very one you have yourself already touched upon in your reference to "artistic feeling". For at the outset of our previous meetings you had explained that for you the typical process of counselling unfolds in seven stages: the stages of preparation, listening and exploration, assimilation, "diagnostic interlude", selection of target area(s), working through the target areas with the client, and finally, helping the client into a new life. Now that was very illuminating, but what I've wondered more and more on reflection is whether the very precision of this articulation of the seven stages could not distract us from the essential thing that keeps the whole process moving along. We could fail to see the wood for the trees.

Let me put it like this. I realise that these ideas evolved in a highly personal way, and yet I cannot help relating them to the ideas of others. You yourself led the way by comparing your sevenfold scheme with the threefold scheme of Stafford-Clark: Receiving; Assimilating; Intervening. And mentally I made the further comparison with the similar threefold scheme of Carkhuff and Egan: Ventilation and Exploration; Understanding; Positive Action. My real interest in bringing together these different universes of discourse, therefore, is to try to put my finger on what is distinctive about your own approach. The surface comparison between your sevenfold scheme and others' threefold scheme is a useful device for beginning to do this. And I've begun to feel that what you were really talking about is a driving force that is embodied in the sevenfold process but that can too easily be lost sight of in the details of this process. And this is something that you referred to in our previous discussions when you occasionally called the whole process "creative", without, however, spelling this out further.

Am I right in thinking there is something on these lines that is for you the essence of the sevenfold scheme?'

'You know, you have almost uncannily homed in on one of my own further reflections on our previous *Gespräche*, conversations. So I'm particularly pleased to try to explain my thoughts on what you have quite rightly perceived is the true driving-force of the counselling process.

I should like to begin by saying that in one sense there's nothing sacrosanct about the number seven. In fact my own sevenfold rhythm could be reduced to a threefold rhythm, the first three stages being concerned with *taking in*, the last three with *giving out*, and the fourth one serving as a point of balance. It would be like breathing in and breathing out, punctuated by a pause and turn. But these are only so many different ways of ordering something which I first experienced as a continuous flow. As I told you before, I practised my particular approach long before I reflected on its process, let alone before discovering that Stafford-Clark had worked out a substantially similar scheme. And I should be quite happy to see them as independent variants of each other.

What I do want to say is that I first lived the experience of counselling and, further, that I lived it as a *human* experience, the experience of two human beings meeting with, engaged with, each other. And perhaps the most important thing of all, as I now realise more clearly, is that all along I've felt and imagined as well as thought of any such real involvement in depth with another human being as a *creative* process. What goes on in a counsellor is for me more like what happens in the composition of a work of art or a piece of music than anything else. It may be a little far-fetched to say that the counsellor is like a creative artist in relation to the client, so let me give a preliminary indication of what I mean.

A serene open-mindedness and objectivity enables the counsellor to absorb a multitude of impressions from his client which come to him unsought in the most varied form, from the most subtle, almost imperceptible, to the most obvious ones. But he will not speculate about them. He will let them sink into the depths of his being, so that they mature there, undisturbed by the interference of his intellect, until in the end they have achieved an organic unity and coherence, a life and being of their own, and reveal their nature and meaning in their own idiom. Understanding and insight into the being of the client and his needs will now dawn on the counsellor, in the same way as the artist or the poet, patient of innumerable subtle impressions, will in the fulness of time be the mouthpiece of the work of art which has matured within him, revealing an, as yet, undiscovered truth and not an arbitrary construction of his intellect. And this is no doubt one reason why I insist that a counsellor should be thoroughly versed in works of art as well as in the ways of the world – I was probably speaking out of the passionate interest I had in frequenting musical concerts in Vienna as a student when I could no longer stand the mechanistic approach to medical studies!

It's this way of looking at counselling that accounts above all, I now think, for anything that's distinctive about my own approach. I also realise more sharply that it's in the *stages of preparation* and then of assimilation that all this is concentrated and comes to expression most of all. You will recall my saying that it's in my opinion critical that a counsellor allows himself time to prepare for the visit of the client, time in which to collect himself and transcend his ordinary intellectual and everyday consciousness. He seeks to tune his whole being to the state of mind which will be necessary for listening to the client. I quoted Steiner's words about thinking "while abstaining from thinking". Essentially the same idea is captured in two further quotations, one from the West and one from the East. Would you be interested in hearing them?'

'I should indeed,' I replied.

'Well, the first is from Carl-Gustav Heyer who, as you may know, was a pupil of Jung, albeit a very independent-minded one. It's an extract from a lecture to his own students which my wife Emma and I translated into English:

Then I did something which, according to my experience, is always to be recommended whenever one is faced with a phenomenon and finds that one has got stuck. Allow me, for the sake of brevity, to put it this way: I did not focus on it, did not look at it energetically, but instead I "blinked". Why just that? In the course of scientific training with its basic attitude, its discoveries, theories and practices, we are accustomed to placing certain facts which have been established into the full light. The gaze of the scientist, whether engaged in research or in practical work, focuses on them. And the more such a scientific tendency is perfected, the brighter these things will get, the darker, however, other things will become, with the result that they will move more and more into the shadow. But if you wish to perceive something which is in the shadow – you know this from walks in the night, from groping through cellars – then you cannot find your orientation by focusing sharply, but by looking through half-closed eyes. For thus those over-bright things which with their dazzling light hide others, are dimmed. That's the sort of thing I mean to describe when I say I "blinked" at the phenomenon. I could also say: I have allowed it to affect me; or: I have behaved in accordance with the old Indian proverb which says: "When someone says to you that he has searched and found, then don't believe him; but the man who tells you that he has not searched, yet found, him you may believe."

This sounds pretty paradoxical to our Western ears and attitudes. I can, however, assure you that in the psychological realms which we will have to deal with, we shall have to acknowledge time and again that *one finds much less through active searching than through allowing things to work on one*, to make their impact on one: through *"blinking"*.

Let me go into this still more specifically, because this passive attitude – as I have said already – plays such a significant part in psycho-therapeutic work; and because, when coming to it from clinical medicine we are used to an utterly different attitude. The psychological process has, to a much higher degree than the somatic process, the character of uniqueness. After all, pneumonia and leg fracture again and again produce a very similar picture and will also to a great extent require similar treatment. In the realm of the physical, human lives are organised in a very similar manner. Therefore in the physical realm, once a few points of reference are established, we may expect to find a diagnosis with some certainty and also to pursue this diagnosis. The position is quite different and much more complicated as soon as the life of the soul is concerned. There the great difference between human beings, according to their inborn qualities, their previous history, their character, becomes obvious and demands full consideration. Certainly I do also know some psycho-therapists who have told me proudly (and, as it seemed to me, in a somewhat bored way) that, after having talked with a patient for five minutes, they already had a clear picture of him; for it was always the same thing anyway ... The same thing? Yes: namely the pattern F, the pattern belonging to some school, to which that therapist had sworn his allegiance and into the framework and conceptual system of which school he had accustomed himself to compress the whole wide variety of life. I may frankly confess to you that I have not yet achieved that sort of pride (nor the boredom connected with it!). Certainly afterwards, after one has seen the whole dramatic event of a human life move past, with all its scenes so rich in colour and full of personages, when one has experienced it again and again, ever anew and always differently – then one will be able and also permitted to classify: here is an hysterical mechanism, there are inferiority anxieties; this is infantile and that is disturbed according to such and such a concept. But if I apply the pattern too early, then I believe I know, and yet in fact I know nothing. For it does not matter for the true understanding and the treatment of a person that I can spell out his diagnosis, but that I learn and, more important still, that he senses it: that his present, highly individual psychological situation is being understood. There it is a question of listening to fine nuances, of being able to be surprised and full of wonder! For it is not what I already know that will necessarily offer me the key to the room of his inner being in order to open up his secret – since the realms and the possibilities of psychological processes are as wide as the world and greater than the sphere of experience of even the most expert individual, it will very often be a matter of sensing and unravelling things which have so far remained unknown, unexplored. Anyone who lets his inquiring eye be blinded and restricted by anticipatory concepts of some doctrine, by preconceived notions, will certainly always find his expectations subjectively confirmed; but whether he will also objectively do justice to the facts, that is an entirely different matter. Therefore we must, in psychotherapeutic work, "blink" very often, so as not on any account to be blinded and diverted by the brightly-lit concepts in the mind of the doctor (*and* in the mind of the client) away from those often more significant events which have their secret life in the background , in the shadow.[2]

I find this quite magnificent and profound, and that is why I have allowed myself to quote it at length. The most significant thing, however, is that he sums up the state of mind and preparedness he advocates in the apparently humble word "blinking": the deliberate dimming down of our ordinary, everyday intellectual consciousness. The other quotation is from an essay about the Indian sage Krishnamurti written by A. Bancroft in her book *Twentieth Century Mystics and Sages*.

He always returns to the same point: that we must die to our conditioning, die to the known past, in order that we can become fully aware of the present which is unknown. This is a dying which can take place moment by moment, he says ... We are afraid to contemplate the Emptiness which might be seen if we ceased to cling. Essentially we cling to the known, which we call life, and are afraid of the unknown.

"So the problem," says Krishnamurti, "is to free the mind from the known, from all the things it has gathered, acquired, experienced, so that it is made *innocent* and can therefore understand that which is death, the unknowable."[3]

You see that the basic endeavour is to achieve a state of innocence in order to understand, which is what I try to do. The key-word, therefore, is "innocent". The connection with "blinking" is obvious.'

'Yes, indeed,' I answered, 'and that is precisely the point I want to take up. But before I do take it up under its main

2. *Der Organismus der Seele*, Ch.1, at p.11. The italics are added.
3. at p.76. The italics are added.

aspect, I should just like to say that I find these quotations as pertinent as they are striking but also that they seem to me to point to a potential state of mind which people keep rediscovering. I began to be aware of this when I read a paper by two psychiatrists, Clancy D. Mackenzie and Lance S. Wright which forms an appendix to *The Silva Mind Control Method* by José Silva and Philip Miele.[4] May I therefore return the compliment and proffer you a quotation?'

'Yes, please do,' replied Dr Gregory.

'I should perhaps preface the quotation by telling you, in case you don't already know, that José Silva is a Texan with no formal education who first discovered within himself – and then over the years developed and finally published to millions, in the manner of an all-American success story – a method of tapping the deepest layers of the mind called the Alpha level, so as to harness them to the use of the conscious mind, referred to as the Beta level. And as I understand it, it is the combination of these two levels, if you like the passivity of the unconscious and the activity of the conscious mind, that warranted the name of "dynamic meditation". His method is measurable by EEG machines and as such takes its place among those many explorations, at once scientific and meditative, which are drawn upon by, say, William Johnston in his *Silent Music*. So here is the quotation from the above-mentioned paper:

> The entire course consists of techniques for using the mind in beneficial ways. After experiencing this ourselves and witnessing many others using it, we have no doubt about the superior ability of the mind to function when the person is using specific techniques in an alert relaxed state. It is similar to the state Sigmund Freud described in his paper on listening; like the state Brahms went into for creating his compositions, or the state Thomas Edison described for arriving at new ideas.[5]

4. 1980.
5. at p.172.

I might add that the state of mind indicated here also seems to be the same as that hit off by one of Freud's most original followers, Wilfred Bion, in his own marvellously teasing phrase "without memory or desire".

Now I think it is interesting to connect all these people from East and West because it suggests, to me at least, that we are dealing with a potentially universal human faculty that is periodically realised only to be lost, time and time again. In other words, we are talking about part of man's birth-right as a human being, and the very fact that it has to be recovered from being lost makes the term you derive from Krishnamurti doubly appropriate: "a state of innocence". It's as if the attainment or recovery of this state of mind were part of the mystery of regaining a more general state of innocence. It seems to be of the order of coming to see "those angel faces smile, which I have loved long since, and lost awhile", as Cardinal Newman put it, or, in the suggestive terminology of Zen Buddhism, of recovering the face one had before one was born, albeit now with effort.

The point, however, is not so much that it requires a sustained habit of will to let drop what one has learned and is inclined to bring to the new situation by way of preconception. The main point is rather that once one has acquired such a fresh receptivity of mind, one can and indeed must *also* use any knowledge one may have. After all, do you not yourself, in fact, allow for these more consciously reflective processes, when you refer to the "diagnostic interlude" and the selection of, and working through, target areas?

I think it's important to see the process as a whole and so better grasp the due and reciprocal role of each part in that whole. There is indeed the effort towards openness, which you are emphasising, but isn't there also the laborious, tangled business of discursive search, trial and error, the passive but also the active, the unconscious but also the conscious? So don't we have to acknowledge *both* the necessary innocence, self-emptying, the deconditioning, which you're talking about, and *also* the ability to use what one has learned in order to structure what one is now taking in, albeit from a new point of view which is appropriate to the present occasion? Do you see?'

'I do take your point, Marcus. You're concerned, as so often, with seeing things as a whole – as I've said before in another context: "seeing things steadily and seeing them whole". I should, however, like to say in my own defence that I did allow for what you call the more conscious and discursive elements, as you've admitted. I just didn't correlate them as explicitly as you have now done. What I wanted to do above all was to bring out the importance of the first process since it is, to my mind, insufficiently appreciated. In fact I should go so far as to say that the second process you've just talked about – the conscious and discursive – will be more or less sterile unless it's preceded by the first process I'm stressing. It's *this process which for me is at the heart of counselling*, and I'm very concerned that it should be properly understood.

The so-called seven stages of counselling should certainly not be taken as a sort of holy cow on account of their relationship to the number seven. Nor should they be taken as just another "method". For me it's a matter of a basic law of life and, more specifically, a basic and inescapable law of *creativity*, rooted in the soil of the "state of innocence". And it's perhaps for this reason that the essence of what I mean has been expressed by creative artists. In particular I have two artists in mind, a poet and a painter.

You may well know the justly celebrated *Letters to a Young Poet* which Rainer Maria Rilke wrote to an aspiring poet. I'll translate the lines I'm thinking of from the German original:

It is all a matter of carrying things to full term and then giving birth. *To allow every impression and every germ of a feeling to come to fullness deep within oneself, in the dark and in the unconscious, below the reach of words and of one's own understanding, and to await the hour of the delivery of a new clarity with humility and patience: this is the only way to live creatively, whether from the point of view of understanding or*

of production ...
Patience is all, *Geduld ist alles*[6]

And there is a fascinating convergent statement about the painter Matisse:

> It is told of Henri Matisse that he gazed at an object which he intended to paint for weeks, for months on end until the spirit within him began to stir and drove him powerfully to bring it to expression. He surrendered himself so completely to such attention that he lost himself more and more in the object. The result of all this was that it was not his ego or his own ideas which painted the object but the object which painted itself through him as its tool. Such works of art are then not just copies, like photographs, they are filled with the very essence of the object.[7]

And for me both these statements have been summed up by somebody who was not an artist in the strict sense of that word but who was, in my opinion, a highly creative presonality. I refer once again to Steiner, who in *Die Welt der Sinne und die Welt des Geistes* wrote as follows (and again I translate myself):

> We should let things themselves speak, hold ourselves more and more passively towards things and allow things to reveal their secrets. We would save a great deal of trouble it we refrained from judgements and let things declare their secrets ...
> Surrender is the attitude of mind according to which one does not want to extract truth from within oneself but expects to gain it from the revelation which streams from things and waits until one is ripe to receive it in this or that particular way.[8]

6. *Briefe an einen jungen Dichter*, at p.19. The italics are added.
7. U. Reiter *Meditation - Wege zum Selbst*, at p.45.
8. at pp.32 and 34.

Do you see? The dynamism of this law, as these three creative people have so well expressed it, is that if we are to live through experience in depth and to make it fruitful, we must absorb the totality of the impressions, the crude as well as the subtle ones inherent in the experience, slowly and patiently. They must be allowed to mature, to ripen in the depths of the soul until they begin, from deep within, to speak their own language, in the way that, as Matisse says of his own medium, the painting begins to paint itself. Only then will the questions within the experience, or, in our case, within the encounter of client and counsellor, lead us gradually to the right responses, attitudes and answers.

That this law of creativity applies universally came home to me with particular force when I was reading a biography of Max Reinhardt, the producer, by Leonhard Fiedler. This is what the author says – I translate from the German:

> One of the characteristics of the producer, however paradoxical it may seem, is *the capacity to stand back and to take in impressions*: "It doesn't do any harm to listen and that way ideas come." The art of attending to, recognising and grasping the kernel of individual performances, to cultivate them and then to integrate them into the harmony of a production is Reinhardt's most frequently reported and most admired quality.[9]

Not only does this quotation show a striking parallel to the creative act of counselling, but this is further highlighted by the fact that Reinhardt was famous for keeping largely silent during rehearsals, predominantly listening, never ostentatiously directing or advising, but occasionally getting up quietly and whispering something into the ear of his actor.

What is more, from all this we can also see more clearly that the counsellor will not be able to make the constantly renewed act of will to clear his mind of preoccupations and preconceptions except as part of a sustained effort to purify and

9. *Max Reinhardt*, at p.38. The italics are added.

transcend himself, which is essentially what I mean by a spiritual life. The operation of the inescapable law of creativity, as I have sought to indicate it, must be made secure by a discipline of a spiritual order. To put it simply, nothing merely subjective or arbitrary must be allowed to intrude.'

'I can completely accept what you're saying, Martin, and I'm glad that you talk about effort and renewal of effort, because this helps to explain a paradox I've experienced. To put it personally, I have sometimes noticed that people seem to absorb a sense of recollection from me and the very room in which I habitually work even when I am, myself, conscious of not much else than distress, tumult and darkness within myself. It's as if we were capable of living at different levels simultaneously and could retain recollection at the deepest level and communicate it from there whatever else is going on inside, *provided* only that there was that serious and strenuous spiritual effort of self-transcendence which you insist on, so that it's from one's deepest desire that one communicates.'

'Yes, I'm talking about something which is hard won and only gradually won, the progressive product of a struggle rather than of anything naturally inherited or induced in the process of nurturing, and I accept completely that we live at different levels. We can, therefore, communicate more than we seem to have at certain given moments. I once had striking personal confirmation of this in the shape of a letter from a young woman I had been seeing and who then wrote to me from abroad. She wrote, amongst other things – I translate from the German: "I don't expect a reply from you, but if you could occasionally include me in your peace and stillness, I should be most grateful." And essentially the same sentiment is expressed in a more universal way by Goethe in his *Iphigenie in Tauris*. Iphigenie is the priestess and she speaks of those troubled by confusion, distress and guilt. I'll read it first in German:

Denken die Himmlischen
Einem der Erdgeborenen

Viele Verwirrungen zu,
Und bereiten sie ihm
Von der Freude zu Schmerzen
Und von Schmerzen zur Freude
Tief-erschuetternden Ubergang;
Dann erziehen sie ihm
In der Naehe der Stadt
Oder am fernen Gestade,
Dass in Stunden der Not
Auch die Huelfe bereit sei,
Einen ruhigen Freund.
O segnet, Goetter, unsern Pylades
Und was er immer unternehmen mag!
Er ist der Arm des Juenglings in der Schlacht,
Des Greises leuchtend Aug in der Versammlung:
Denn seine Seele ist stille; sie bewahrt
Der Ruhe heiliges unerschoepftes Gut,
Und den Umhergetriebnen reichet er
Aus ihren Tiefen Rat und Huelfe   (IV, 2)

Roughly translated, this means:

If the heavenly beings destine one of the earth-born to
many confusions and mean him to experience violent
swings from joy to pain and from pain to joy, they also
make sure that, near the town or in some remote place,
help is available in the hours of need – *a serene friend.* O
Gods, bless our Pylades and all he undertakes! He is the
arm of youth in battle, the piercing eye of venerable age
in assembly: for *his soul is still. He retains the sacred,
inexhaustible good of peace* and from its depths he offers
help and counsel to the bewildered and the driven.

It will not escape you that the peace which is in question is not
only personal peace, something at least striven for by the
individual, but a peace which comes from elsewhere, beyond
ourselves, and that it comes not so much from what we do but

from what we are and are given.'

'So what you're bringing out is the idea that peace can be transmitted from one person to another, caught by one from another. But can't we take this a little further and say that creativity too can and needs to be communicated to the other? For what you've been talking about so far is the way in which a veritably creative process of assimilation and maturing akin to gestation takes place – or should take place – within the *counsellor*. But the counsellor is there in order to help the client so that his processes must be made to serve the client, and this in turn suggests the thought that the creative process should at least in some measure spread to the client in a sort of healthy contagion *so that the client, too, slowly learns to live from his own deeper resources.* Don't we have to say that the creative attitude you've been indicating, in principle, becomes a joint and shared process?'

'Indeed we do, Marcus, and what's involved is summed up for me in a little incident in the life of Fritz Busch, the conductor. For it's like the relationship between an orchestra and the conductor. Every conductor, you will know, has to beat time, but it's the difference between the sound achieved by the great conductor, often with just a few gestures or glances, and the lesser one, with a great deal of exertion, which convinces me that there is an almost telepathic relationship between orchestra and conductor, from the word go, and this works both ways. Thus, in the incident I'm thinking about, Fritz Busch was rehearsing the overture to *Figaro* at Glyndebourne when the violinists lifted their instruments and he said: "Already too loud." You see, the tiniest gesture, the very mood spoke between them.'

'I appreciate the example, and, you know, in the face of so many of your ideas which derive part of their potency from being so condensed and suggestive, I sometimes feel a little guilty about exposing them to the clumsy touch of my own analytic mind. But as long as we can appreciate the complementarity of each other's mentalities, we can, I hope, proceed with mutual enrichment.'

'I certainly feel that,' Dr Gregory rejoined.

'Well then, Martin, if that's so, may I take the thrust of our exploration a little further yet, on lines you've already suggested.

Where we began was your insistence that counselling is a creative process, more like a work of art than anything else. You went on to explain that this creativity is concentrated in the stages of preparation and then of assimilation in so far as this consists in a state of mind which can variously be called receptive, unconditioned, innocent.'

'Yes, my point is that this willed and disciplined abstention from thinking is *the precondition* for allowing the other's being and situation to mature within him in the way in which a creative artist allows the work of art to live a life of its own.'

'Just so, Martin. We then agreed that the "state of innocence" was less a matter of achievement than of striving on the part of the counsellor and that it was precisely in this respect that he could emit a certain peace. And from there I went on to suggest that creativity too could be communicated in a similar way. So we're saying that the being of the counsellor is more important than any doing of his, even that any such more active involvement must be anchored in his being; and that he can sometimes emit a greater peace than he himself feels at the time; and finally that the, as it were, alchemy of change in the client consists in large part in the catching of this creativity. But in saying all this, aren't we pointing to some further truth?

You see, when you showed me Udo Reiter's book and the passage about Matisse I noticed a few further lines down the same page that the author quoted Matisse himself – may I have the book back for a moment:

> Art begins in real earnest when one no longer under-stands what one is doing and what one can do and yet detects a power within oneself which grows stronger the more one resists it. One therefore has to keep oneself completely clear, pure and innocent for it.

Now Matisse's own mention of a "power" working in and through the artist and the author's complementary talk of the artist being a "Werkzeug", a tool or instrument, suggest that there is something beyond the individual being creative from his own resources alone. Matisse comes to stand in the line of Socrates who spoke of being inspired by a *daemon*, some inbreathing from outside. But this means in turn that where another is progressively gathered into such a process of creativity, there is something beyond both of them. So aren't we saying in effect that the process of the *Gespräch*, the dialogue, could be redescribed as an invitation by the counsellor to the client to join in the process more and more as an equal partner and therefore as the communication of the effort of self-transcendence from one person to the other until both are acting together but also receiving some common thing together, which is therefore greater than either? Could we even say that they are in the joint service of some common thing? In other words the counsellor seems, not so much to impart, as to mediate, not so much to give as to initiate into some larger process. Aren't we revealed to be not so much even agents of transformation, as vehicles – along the lines on which Mozart, despite, and in his very humanity, was seen at last by his rival Salieri to be a carrier of the silent "music of the spheres", truly *amadeus*, cherished by God?

And the point of venturing to draw out your insights in this way is that it brings us full circle and enables us to see at a deeper level why counselling is what you have for long seen and said it is: a creative process. We begin to grasp how it can be seen to be part of a cosmic process. Here I'm reminded of the almost final words of Esther Harding in *The Way of All Women* – which incidentally also relates the process of counselling back to ordinary life:

> In every act of sexual intercourse, the woman implicitly accepts her role as servant in the Temple of Life ...
> In the recognition that man does not live for himself alone even in his most individual and personal acts – not

even in his relation to the one person in all the world whom he loves – in this recognition the truly religious spirit is born. The most precious things of life do not belong to us personally. In our most intimate acts, our most secret moments, we are *lived* by Life. Again and again we are reminded that in the daily contact with one we love our little personal egos must be surpassed; only so *can we take our place in the stream of life and submit ourselves to that suprapersonal value* which alone can give significance and dignity to the individual. For when two people experience each other unmasked – in stark reality – emotional energy which has had its counterpart in the past only in religious experience is in modern times released and made available for human development.[10]'

'You know, Marcus, I'd never seen it quite like this, and yet I have for some time now been dimly aware of some of the cosmic associations of my sevenfold scheme.'

'Yes, what we seem to have stumbled on is the intuition that – at its deepest and best – the counselling process is a reproduction at the inter-personal level of the creative process on the world level. This is why it's better spoken of as process transcending the narrowly personal, and since the world's evolutionary process is directed and so goal-seeking and future-orientated, isn't this also the reason why you have also long seen that the counselling process must be future-orientated? So perhaps we ought to take up this theme and develop it along these lines?'

'I should love to do so', said Dr Gregory, 'but on another occasion, please.'

'Very good, I'll hold you to that.'

10. At pp.275 and 276. The italics are added.

Dialogue 2:
Backwards and
Forwards

But how is it
That this lives in thy mind? What seeest thou else
In the dark backward and abysm of time?
> Shakespeare *The Tempest* Act I Scene 2

If you can look into the seeds of time,
And say which grain will grow and which will not,
Speak then to me, who neither beg nor fear
Your favours nor your hate.
> Shakespeare *Macbeth* Act I Scene 3

'I'd like to take up where we left off last time, Martin. We were exploring your conviction that counselling should be seen, above all, as a creative process and we ended up by agreeing that it was ultimately creative because it was part of the larger creative process of the cosmos. We concluded with the thought that these greater processes were directed, and so future-oriented, that the counselling process should, therefore, as a reflection of them, share the same feature. I know that this is something else you are quite convinced of. I realise that you are essentially right, and yet I cannot shake off certain perplexities. It is not just that a great deal of therapy seems to be concerned with interrogating the past in order to reassess and reconstruct it, that there has been talk of controlled regression and, even more recently, a great interest in re-birthing and the primal scream. There seems to be a feeling about in at least some therapeutic circles that if only we can return to the origin of our ills, we can begin to imagine and feel an alternative.

In this connection I think it is significant, not only of the tendency in pychoanalysis and its derivations, but of its popularisation that an interview with Donald Winnicott should have been published almost twenty years ago now in the *Observer* Sunday Colour Supplement. The interviewer put an objection: "How do you *know* a baby feels like that about the breast? It can't tell you, it doesn't remember later." He said, "When you get badly disturbed patients under analysis they don't just tell you things, they actually *become* what they've been – they sit there and mess themselves and cry, they suck milk off your fingers." I said, "But these people are not normal people – how much can that tell you about normal babies?" After a bit, he said, "It's the most wonderful thing – they begin to show you *how it could have gone right*".[1]

Now personally I find that these last few words have the simplicity and the ring of truth of so much of Winnicott's writings, though the credit of the real pioneer must once again go to Freud. At the same time, your stress on future-orientation also feels right, and I associate this tendency with, apart from yourself, Professor Eugene Heimler, who, interestingly enough, is also a Jew. Perhaps the contrast between Freud and Heimler represents a polarity in the Jewish psyche. Be that as it may, Eugene Heimler, as you may know, belongs to that band of survivors from the holocaust of Auschwitz and Belsen who made of it a crucible of creativity and deep insight into human nature, people like Bruno Bettelheim and Victor Frankl. And one of Heimler's main convictions is that people need to be helped to work towards the future and that it is the success in coping with the present that sets in train a new feel and view about the past, not the other way round.

My problem, therefore, is whether the counsellor should work on the past or the future, go backwards or forwards; if you like, whether Freud or Heimler is right.'

'Once again, Marcus, you've touched one of the nerves of

1. 25 September 1966, at p.20. The italics are added.

my thinking, because I am quite convinced, as you say, that the main business of the counsellor is to open up the client to the future. I can sum up my meaning in terms of an experience which has come to be a significant image for me.'

'Part of your personal mythology?'

'Yes, part of my personal mythology. Well, you know that I used to love walking down towards Crammond. In this way I observed that the little harbour was usually clogged with various bits of debris and that the River Almond which opened out into it at that point was usually too sluggish to move any of that junk. Every now and then, however, the river would gain power and sweep away a great deal of all this deposit from the past out into the sea. Not that everything would of course be removed in this way. It might be driven into the bed of the river, but in any case it was not an obstruction any more. It was this fact of nature that became an image for me of the way in which life can become obstructed but also renewed. If we can only help people to release the energies of life that are directed to the future, most of the blockages in the way will simply be swept away.

Now I realise that such release of energies and drive towards the future represents a *second* phase after what I should call a more quiescent and introspective phase. Nobody can make the effort of release who is totally wrapped up with his past and he needs a lot of patient care to be freed of his emotional burdens and his sense of guilt and failure. This initial phase is no doubt what corresponds to the analytic process as you have evoked it in your references to Winnicott and Freud. Only I don't call this phase analytic, because, quite frankly, I've never experienced it in this way.

In the first place, the very term "analytic" sounds too mechanistic, suggesting as it does to me chemical analysis and search for something specific, some flaw.

Why else do I find the analytic approach unhelpful? I was puzzled about this, and I've come up with a tentative answer. It seems to me now that such an approach was quite appropriate in Freud's age, for it was a repressive age in which so much was driven underground. I know it, because I experienced it, I was there, I knew about the family situation and about little Jewish boys sleeping with their mothers and the Oedipus conflict, and so on. But so much has changed since then. Our age is not repressive. On the contrary, we have, in sexual matters, found a new freedom. A freedom we can't yet control. Young people are marvellously free and are aspiring souls, and yet they flounder because they don't have discipline and insight. So when I deal with young people, as I've been doing for a long time now, I don't need to unearth what's been buried – it's all out in the open. What I experience is a mass of shadows, guilt and failure, and above all error, misjudgement. It is significant that in the teaching of the Buddha, who, after all, knew human beings very well, the source of all ills was the failure to comprehend reality as it is. So what I have to do is to help people to see things as they actually are – as Goethe puts it in a beautiful little poem, "sich ins Recht denken", to think oneself into the right outlook.

So what I do is doubtless no easier that what analysts do, but it is different in character. I do not search for the deep-seated unconscious block, because for most people *it isn't there*, but I do need to clear away all sorts of mistaken notions, wrong judgement, errors. But once we have cleared these away and people can begin to emerge from the twilight guilt-ridden zone with a measure of self-respect, we can begin to work on releasing the river of life, energy.

Here I should like to bring to your attention two quotations which made a great impression on me. The first is taken from Prabhavananda and Isherwood's account of the teaching of Patanjali, the classical exponent of the yoga system, in their book *How to Know God – The Yoga Aphorisms of Patanjali*. They begin by quoting the third aphorism in Book IV of the Yoga Sutras themselves, on liberation, and then add their own comment:

3. Good or bad deeds are not the direct causes of the transformation. They act only as breakers of the obsta-

cles to natural evolution; just as a farmer breaks down the obstacles in a water course, so that water flows through by its own nature.

Here Patanjali explains the Hindu theory of evolution of species by means of an illustration from agriculture. The farmer who irrigates one of his fields from a reservoir does not have to fetch the water. The water is there already. All the farmer has to do is to open a sluice gate or break down a dam, and the water flows into the field by the natural force of gravity.

The "water" is the force of evolution which, according to Patanjali, each one of us carries within him, only waiting to be released from the "reservoir". By our acts we "open the sluice gate", the water runs down into the field, the field bears its crop and is thereby transformed ... "All progress and power are already in every man," says Vivekenanda. "Perfection is in every man's nature, only it is barred in and prevented from taking its proper course. If anyone can take the bar off, in rushes nature."[2]

Of course the therapist himself can't take the bar off, the client has to do that: "You can take the horse to water, but you can't make it drink." The therapist can, however, alert the client to the existence of the bar.

So man is by his nature future-oriented and must – and wants – to go forwards. At the same time he can make this effort only once he has been liberated to say Yes to this effort.

My second quotation is from Goethe. You will know that he was a universal man, but he went through very great crises and struggles and experienced much illness. The secret of his survival was "tätig sein", to be active, so that a general statement of his outlook is really autobiographical. This is what he says in *Wilhelm Meister*:

To heal psychic ailments that we have contracted

2. at p.204.

through misfortune or faults of our own,
ing avails nothing, reason little, time mu
activity everything.[3]

I don't go all the way with Goethe here
understanding can avail, but I do agree wit
activity. So we're back to setting a person
towards a goal, being motivated to lead w
the "logotherapist", calls a "life of meaning'

'You've said a great deal there alr
particularly captivated by the way you'v
drum experience of the River Almond
significance by associating it with Patanjal
What you're saying is that the therapist's
to enable the release of this stream of
sluice-gate or removing the obstacle in th
flow. At the same time you've indicated th
stream of life is the second phase of a pr
begin with what you call a more "quiescent and introsp
phase" and which you say corresponds to Freud's analytic
work. It's at this point that I'd like to come in, because the
very juxtaposing of your emphasis on the future with Freud's
delving into the past leaves my initial problem intact: Should
the therapist and client go forwards or backwards and, if in
some sense both, then how and in what proportion? Do you
see my puzzle?'

'I do Marcus, and I'm not sure that I can resolve it at
present. I wonder, however, whether it would help it I
illustrated what I've said rather generally with a few concrete
cases?'

'That could be very useful, Martin. Please go ahead.'

'Well, then, my first case is taken from the significantly
entitled *New Pathways in Psychology: Maslow and the Post-
Freudian Revolution* by Colin Wilson, who had a personal
contact with Maslow and wrote this book after the latter's
death. The essential theme of the book, as you may know, is

3. Quoted *Goethe, Wisdom and Experience* ed. N.J. Weigand, at p.215.

that the first, and certainly the second generation after Freud began to turn away from preoccupation with the past towards a greater attention to the future and, incidentally, in this respect rejoined Jung in one of his major concerns.'

'You know, I had thought that this revolution, as you call it, had already started with Karen Horney in America, Martin?'

'That may be, I just don't know. All I do know is that any prior tendency in that direction became more pronouced and explicit with Maslow. So here is the first of the cases as presented by Colin Wilson, in a paper called "The Need to Know and the Fear of Knowing", Maslow describes one of his crucial cases.

"Around 1938, a college girl patient presented herself complaining vaguely of insomnia, lack of appetite, disturbed menstruation, sexual frigidity, and a general malaise which soom turned into a complaint of boredom with life and an inability to enjoy *anything* ... As she went on talking, she seemed puzzled. She had graduated about a year ago and by a fantastic stroke of luck – this was the depression, remember – she had immediately got a job, and what a job! Fifty dollars a week! She was taking care of her whole unemployed family with the money and was the envy of all her friends. But what was the job? She worked as a sub-personnel manager in a chewing-gum factory. After some hours of talking, it became more and more clear that she felt she was wasting her life. She had been a brilliant student of psychology and was very happy and successful in college, but her family's financial situation made it impossible for her to go on into graduate studies. She was greatly drawn to intellectual work, not altogether consciously at first because she felt she *ought* to feel fortunate with her job and the money it brought her. Half-consciously then she saw a whole lifetime of greyness stretching out ahead of her. I suggested that she might be feeling profoundly frustrated and angry simply because she was not being her own very intellectual self, that she was not using her intelligence and her talent for psychology and that this might well be a major reason for her boredom with life and her body's boredom with the normal pleasures of life. Any talent, any capacity, I thought, was also a motivation, a need, an impulse. With this she agreed, and I suggested that she could continue her graduate studies at night after her work. She became more alive, more happy and zestful, and most of her physical symptoms had disappeared at my last contact with her."

It is significant that Maslow, although trained as a Freudian, did not try to get back into the subject's childhood and find out whether she experienced penis-envy of her brothers or a desire to murder her mother and marry her father. He followed his instinct – his feeling that creativeness and the desire for a *meaningful existence* are as important as any subconscious sexual drives.[4]

Now I personally find the facts so simple that you would have to be a fool not to leave aside the subsidiary symptoms – the boredom, insomnia, sexuality etc. – and not go straight for the central thing in the present. The case does, however, make the essential point.'

'It's a paradigm of Maslow's approach?' I asked.

'Yes, he worked with the concept of *meaning*, much as Victor Frankl did, although his own preferred term is self-actualisation, which sums up his notion of man being a forward-moving, growing, developing, integrating personality. It is this characteristic which dominates everything else, because for him – as also for me, if I may say so – this represents man's basic impulse, although it can, of course, be dammed up, as Patanjali had already observed.

So we come to my own two cases.

The first case is that of what I call the "Irish Girl". She was referred to me by the Samaritans, and turned out to be

4. at pp.22 and 23.

typically Irish, blue-eyed, black-haired. She was married to an Egyptian doctor. The problem was that of a total breakdown of the marriage at every level. I saw her and she was miserable. The next thing I did was to see her husband – I feel that one can't solve any marriage problem without dealing with both partners, simply because one can't rely on the description of somebody emotionally distressed. He turned out to be a gentle, sweet-natured and talented man, who couldn't understand what was the matter. When I saw the Irish girl again, I discovered that she had trained as a nurse but was now sitting at home and had become what I call a "captive wife". After some discussion she ventured to mention that she would like to study medicine, but this seemed to be too far-fetched and adventurous. I saw the husband again, and he said it was fine by him, provided it was practically possible. Well, it was possible, and from that moment the whole thing resolved itself like magic. They left the country, and they wrote to me at Christmas saying that she had started her medical career and they were very happy. So that's a simple case of breaking out of captivity into freedom.

The next case was not quite so simple. It involved a young homosexual man who worked in a factory. What initially bothered him was his sexual isolation but what came over above all was his total cultural deprivation, a veritable dehydration and emptiness of life. To cut a long story short, I discovered that he liked music, and he developed an interest in opera. He became so enthusiastic that whenever the opera came to town he was the first in the queue for tickets at the box office. From then on, the whole feel of his life changed. He began to have a glow, an enthusiasum. He didn't cease to be a homosexual, but he felt that there was something in his life, something to look forward to, something which could develop, and he became able to talk with women by way of a simple human exchange. The total concentration on his homosexuality was dissipated, simply by virtue of the fact that he had discovered opera. Then things gained momentum and he developed other interests as well.'

'He found a goal?'

'Yes, and self-respect.

'The final case is strictly not my own but one of Bridget's, which I discussed with her. Again a marriage was in crisis. The man was highly intelligent and in a good position, and the woman was very simple, almost mentally-handicapped; she could hardly cope with her domestic situation. In addition their one son was deaf. The whole situation was very confined. She could give her husband little enough, sexually, culturally, humanly, but he was attached to her and they got on surprisingly well, except in one respect. He had one great wish, namely that she should perform erotic dances – which is fairly common after all. But how on earth could a woman who was so handicapped and helpless oblige? You could as easily imagine an elephant dancing as this poor woman.'

'A complete impasse?'

'An impasse. What to do? So Bridget came to discuss the situation with me. I asked her whether there was anything the woman could do. It appeared that there was *one* thing she could and liked to do, which was to make dresses, but even that she did very badly. Well, perhaps she could learn to make them a little better? So Bridget arranged for her to have dress-making lessons, and I suggested that the woman should make it really purposeful and aspire to make beautiful dresses. She was enthusiastic. It gave her endless pleasure to be able to make something beautiful for herself.'

'But did she learn to perform the erotic dances?'

'The long and the short of the story is that she *was* able to perform erotic dances for her husband, and I when I last asked Bridget about her, she said "Oh, she's come a long way since then – she's branching out".'

'These cases do illustrate your thesis very well, Martin,' I said, 'and it is very appealing. Yet I have to say that questions remain in my own mind. In the first place, I doubt whether our age is as different from Freud's as you make out. I personally find in my work both as priest and as counsellor that a lot of us are still riddled with guilt and fear and repression, especially in matters sexual, and that those brought up in the Protestant and Catholic traditions suffer only variants of essentially similar hang-ups.

At a more theoretical level my impression of even the psychoanalytic tradition of therapy is, on the one hand, that psychoanalysts are essentially as concerned with the present and the future as you are, and on the other hand, that the attention they give to origins and development, to what Melanie Klein well called "the roots of adult life in infancy",[5] is justifiable.

More personally, I should say that I have through my own analysis moved from an apparent preoccupation with the past to emerge to a conception of a very subtle interaction between past, present and future. In this conception we are, in therapy as in life, always concerned with coping with the present and with blockages to such coping here and now. We therefore attend to the past only in so far as the problems in the present prove to be versions or reactivations of maladjustments, traumas, displacements, circumventions, compensations, distortions, what have you, in a past in which one gradually discovers that "it could have gone right", it could have been otherwise, as Winnicott so succinctly put it. This is surely because we forget nothing, everything is there, so that coming back to what appears to be the origin in the past is in fact coming to a point of choice and growth in one's *present* resources. Birth is a metaphor of rebeginning *now*.

My initial problem, therefore, still remains. Only I should, in view of what you have said, now put the problem a little differently: Let us grant the importance of releasing people into the future, as you stress; let us grant further also the therapeutic value of becoming aware of where difficulties in the present began, especially in view of your admission that the phase of moving into the future is preceded by a "more quiescent and introspective" phase – then what is the relative weight of these two phases, how do they interconnect?'

'You do press me, Marcus, don't you? But it's probably

5. *Our Adult World and its Roots in Infancy* (1960)

good for me. And since you do, I must say that I abhor "method" as a preconceived pattern of approach to interpreting the infinitely varying manifestations of life, as I hope I've made clear before. However, by saying this I don't wish to be taken for a kind of dreamer drifting on the waves of what one might benevolently call "imagination". I trust that by now I've made it sufficiently clear that, although I dislike any so-called "method", yet I am totally committed to identifying, in a disciplined way, with the processes of growing, unfolding and forward-moving life, as it expresses itself in the seven stages of counselling, on the lines we have discussed in our previous series of conversations. Naturally, no single element should be made sacrosanct. That would be lapsing into dogmatism. Therefore, if I have any method at all, it is based on the trust that, if I fully submit to this discipline and if I am able to exercise restraint and patience, then life itself will guide me – it may be forwards, it may be backwards, to use your terminology – and will eventually, in the fullness of time, give me the answers. If this sounds rather like poetic language to you and reminds you of a process of fulfilment, like waiting patiently for the fruit to ripen or like gestation, then, yes, you are right: the analogy is valid. Incidentally, I'm encouraged in this aversion to "method" by discovering that I share it with none other than Jung. He said: "The doctor and observer must be free from every formula to allow the living reality to work upon him in its entire lawless richness ... It is therefore wise of the physician to renounce all premature assumptions ... When it comes to things like these, everything depends on the man and little or nothing on method."[6]

Thus I believe passionately in releasing the river of life into the future, and yet I do recognise that there are times when you have to go back. Then you may get the sense of what I call *ungelebtes Leben*, unlived life, from a client, a life or a period of life which has not been lived through. Let me give you an illustration. I was seeing a fine, happily married mother of five children, a woman of forty-two, for the first time. Prior to

6. From *A Jung Anthology* ed. Jolande Jacobi, at p.71.

seeing me she had gone through a period of extreme anxiety. I took her biography, as I usually do. She had done her nurse's training, started nursing and then married at twenty-six, one event following the other in very quick succession. I lived with this story, as I always do, without any particular idea of the outcome, without brooding, just letting the events follow each other within me. In this way I gradually began to feel that something was missing from her life, that she had not had the opportunity for freedom and experience which I have found young people need in order to discover life and the world and so themselves. So, towards the end of the next session, I told her that I had the impression that her life had gone rather rapidly, and asked her whether she felt she had missed out on anything. She said easily enough that she had not, then she suddenly became thoughtful and said: "Now that you mention it, I remember that just before I married I had the strong feeling that I ought to take a year out, but I didn't and I felt I should have done." That was it. You see, you can only be future-orientated if your past is in order, if you have lived through the phases you need to live through – which, of course, varies from one individual to another.'

'That's all I need to hear you say, Martin. Now that you have made the essential concession I felt was necessary, you've made it in a marvellously telling phrase: *"unlived life"*. In two words you sum up the reason for what you call the initial "quiescent and introspective" phase and for a great deal of the work of psychoanalysts. It's to the extent that we all, to a greater or lesser extent, have parts of our life outstanding, still due to be lived, as it were, that we need to put them in order, as you put it, before being able to move on. It's like an advancing army that leaves pockets of resistance behind it needing to be mopped up; the question is when and how it is to do so.'

'Yes, the question is how one is to rectify such a situation. In the case I mentioned the ideal solution would have been for the woman to go to Paris to bask in the arts which she loved so much, feeling "This is me", for the six or even twelve months she should have had almost twenty years earlier. But how could she do this now with five children? What was more feasible was to go for one month. That would be a compromise. You see, to my mind, there are ideal solutions, compromise solutions and there are token solutions.'

'You think that somebody who discovers this "unlived life" like this must live it through, act it out in some way, do you, Martin? Wouldn't it be enough simply to recognise the need, realise it and face it internally alone?'

'Perhaps once again there is no general answer, but only a series of individual answers. What my experience has convinced me of is that, if a person has a burning need, it becomes part of his destiny to face it, and sometimes at least the very fact that he has expressed the need and realised the problem may resolve it. He may be able to go back to ordinary life and say: "I can carry on now." In any case the question is whether the accumulation of unlived life has been mentally, psychologically discharged or not.'

'By so fully and vividly allowing for this as it were debt from the past – perhaps the ontological *Schuld*, guilt/debt of Heidegger – you have allayed my misgiving about the one-sideness of an exclusive concentration on the future.

I hope you will not think me captious to put to you another difficulty that has come to me as you were speaking. I want not so much to test you as to draw out further implications of what you are saying. Let me put my new difficulty like this. You speak fairly consistently of the counsellor listening, exploring, understanding, correcting errors and misjudgements, *knowing*, whereas I'm more and more convinced from the experience of myself as well as of others, that change, release, action is a matter of *feeling* much more than of *knowing*. More and more often I've had people echo my own question: "Yes, I understand, but what am I to *do*?" Once again this problem is not confined to us. Even such usually clear-headed summarisers of the heritage of Freud as Sandler, Dare and Holder in their admirably succint and informative book *The Patient and the Analyst*[7] flounder when they seek to sort out the concept of "insight"[8]. Is it a matter of cognition or of affect, or somehow both? "The major problem in the psychoanalytic literature following Freud appears to lie in the need to define the qualities which distinguish 'true' or 'emotional' insight on the one hand and purely intellectual insight on the other."[9]

'Yes, that's a very fair question, Marcus. I should like to begin to try to respond by saying that the interchange between therapist and client is for the therapist a matter of *knowing*, perceiving clearly where the client has got bogged down what prevents him from seeing reality as it is. The client for his part will then gradually *feel* different.'

'The therapist's effort to understand will somehow communicate itself to the client in terms of feeling? Is that what you're saying?'

'Yes, it will, so to speak, deposit itself in the client in the form of feeling. It's not so much that he'll think that he's wrong in this or that way, it's rather that he'll feel different, which is an existential thing. These things are very subtle and difficult to analyse. I come back to saying with Jung that the process is like a work of art: there is an infinite number of ways of composing a symphony or painting a picture. The particular emphasis must vary from case to case. I'm dealing, for instance, at the moment with a young fellow who feels that he's a failure. This is at the most a partial truth. For my part, I have to see, in a cognitive sense, where he's failed himself, but I have to be very careful not to explain too much to him, especially as he's a pretty intellectual fellow. What I do have to do is to appeal to his feelings and give him the feeling that he already is something, somebody. Now he happens to be a tall figure of a man with magnificent long flowing blonde hair. So we were talking loosely and casually about a number of things, and at one point I told him, which is true: "You remind me of one of those Wagnerian tenors I got to know and admire as a

7. (1979)
8. at pp.115-120.
9. at p.118.

young man at the Vienna Opera." You see, this speaks to him and gives him the feeling that this is how he appears to people, that there is something attractive about him. So although the cognitive and the emotional are theoretically distinct, I try as it were to translate what I know into what he can feel, I try to reach out into the possibilities of the future at that level. There is, in practice, a constant intermingling of these aspects with a view to helping the client to *do* something with his life.

In this connection, you will remember that I've tended to speak of my approach in terms of a *Gesprächstherapie*, a dialogue therapy, whereas the dialogue is only half of the story and I ought more strictly to be speaking of *action*-therapy as well as action towards the future motivated by feeling. We need, at first, to be content with little things, not concerning ourselves straightway with long-term objectives. For instance, this young man mentioned that he would like to sing but felt very uncertain about his voice. So I said: "Look, I'm not a concert preformer, but I can sit down at the piano and tinkle away, so next time let's try out your voice." Something begins to move. Little by little we may be able to help self-confidence and a new feeling about the self to grow, always playing it by ear and finding the right tone. Does that answer your question, Marcus?'

'I certainly get the feel of what you're saying, Martin, and perhaps I ought to be content with that, but by now you'll know that I'm incorrigibly analytic and always want to make further "raid[s]" on the inarticulate as T.S. Eliot puts it – try to give more adequate and precise expression to the almost indefinable things of life. While you were talking, another way of rendering what you call the intermingling of processes came to me. Your phrase "something begins to move" says the essential thing. For don't we need to push the analysis of what goes on within and between counsellor and client back to the mere fact of their being together at all in so far as this embodies their wanting to move? Doesn't the very coming together imply that they are already on the move? Their "working alliance", the fact that both desire something –

although they may well not yet know what – is what enables even "mere" understanding to act at least as the removal of an obstacle to the impetus of the flow and therefore to have an emotional effect. To recur to your master-image, what is in question is not the flow but the blocking by the sluice-gate. What's in question is not, shall we say, libido in its etymological meaning of liking, loving, longing, being inclined, attracted, but what impedes it. So as soon as the blockage is removed, the potential flow is realised anew. So perhaps we need to supplement the image of the water dammed up behind the sluice-gate with the image of two travellers, two mountaineers perhaps, negotiating obstacles in their paths, so that the question between them is not whether but, *presupposing the movement*, how the movement is to be effected. Or, to recur to the perhaps even more basic simile, the good parent's seeking to help the child help itself presupposes the child's own capacity and wish to get going again. Isn't it the pervasive presence of this endeavour or inclination that provides the "affective framework" which Sadler, Dare and Holder say needs to be provided in therapy and within which anything done by and between the counsellor and the client can be productive of movement and thereby change? Put more philosophically, where there is already movement, an "is" is in fact an "ought" – endeavour in the strict sense of en-devoir.'

'That way of seeing things certainly accords with my approach, Marcus, but, as so often, you have put it in a larger, almost a metaphysical way which, as you know very well, is just not my own thing.'

'Flattery will get you nowhere, Martin! More seriously, I'm encouraged by your ready acceptance of my difficulties to present yet another one! So far we've agreed that we must take account not only of the forward drive but of any drag of the past, and we've elucidated a little further the process of dealing with the "unlived life" so as to release the flow of life forward again. What I should now like to do is to essay a unified account which does justice to both these dimensions and, in particular, to the way they interconnect and intermingle in the living, very variable process of therapy.'

'Well, all I can do is to try to express how I handle things. For me there are definitely two elements: there is basically the forward drive, but there may also be various "Hemmungen", obstructions, and there may be what I call "unlived life". Now I bear both in mind, but I deal with the past, the obstruction or the unlived life, *in the light of the future*. To return to the woman of forty-two I was mentioning earlier, it was not just a matter of her doing what she might have done earlier; it was a matter of realising something unfulfilled which belonged to her nature but doing so in such a way that it led into the future. In another case it might have been a question of going back to have a love affair. That may well be necessary, but it can also be dangerous, even destructive. But if there is a forward drive already, the ego-forces will be in control to a greater or lesser extent. It all depends on whether people live through it in a positive and active way. To my mind, *any recapitulation – of education, culture, sex, whatever – which may be necessary needs to be done with mindfulness of the life as a whole, thoughtfully.*'

'Within a perspective of the future?'

'Yes, Marcus, within the perspective of the whole life.'

'So what you're saying, Martin, is, in my own words, that it may be useful and necessary to distinguish intellectually between successive phases in a single process of therapy, but that in concrete reality the potential for self-direction towards the future is present from the very beginning, even though it may for some time appear only fragmentarily and fitfully. The answer to my problem is, therefore, that the two phases are phases of emergence or manifestation rather than of distinct and unrelated existence. The counsellor must, therefore, be aware of this from the beginning, and to the extent that he is aware of this potential even when dealing with more immediate conflicts and inhibitions and pain, he will deal with them only as part of mobilising the future-oriented forces and so give assistance to every such movement into the future.'

'Yes I can completely agree with this statement of what you call a unified view of the intermingling of the movements forwards and backwards. The point is that we cannot face the past and its pain without having something else to look forward to, and I in my turn should just like to sum this up in my own way with three more of my favourite quotations since they have, for a long time, sounded the depths of man's great destiny and goal for me.

You may or may not have heard of Dr Friedrich Rittelmeier who was co-founder of the Christian community. Be that as it may, he had this to say in the last sermon he preached:

Ein Ich is uns anvertraut, ein hoch herrliches Gut –

"An I is entrusted to us, a great and glorious good."[10] A treasure is given into our care and keeping, something to guard, cherish, develop, a promise of a great future.

The second quotation is from the nineteenth century poet Christian Morgenstern, whom I have referred to before. He wrote:

Es soll des Menschen Bildnis wachsen
Und alles andere gilt mir nichts –

"Man's true image must grow within him, and besides that nothing else matters for me."[11]

The last quotation will be familiar to you; it is from St Paul's letter to the Colossians:

I became a minister according to the divine office which was given to me for you, to make the word of God fully known, the mystery from ages and generations but now made manifest to the saints. To them God chose to make known how great among the gentiles are the riches of this mystery, which is *Christ in you, the hope of glory.*[12]

10. *Die Christengemeinschaft* (1938), 'Letzte Predigt'
11. *Epigramme und Sprüche* (1922), at p.113.
12. 1 : 25-27

For me, then, an evolutionary expectation, an instinct and a hope, a purposeful thrust, lives within every man, making for coherence amidst forces of disintegration. This is what makes man's existence a being that is directed towards the realisation of his final end, his perfection. Goethe called it entelechy, from the Greek word *telos*, end: having an end within one. The crucial thing is that the inner direction of this dynamic is beyond his limited being. The essence of the forward drive is towards man's higher self, the Christ in us.

It seems to me that man in his higher self subconsciously or superconsciously wants to be part of the whole forward movement of the cosmic process. So once the process of liberation from conflict, error, illusions is under way, a person becomes aware in his higher being that his personality partakes in the destiny of the whole earth. I believe too that this is not merely a speculative but a vitally practical matter in so far as these things have begun and will continue to break more and more into the lives of more and more people.

This, then, is the substance of the thing. But it has for me all sorts of expressions. May I indicate some of the ways in which I see this dynamic and expectation operating?'

'By all means, Martin. Now that I've got your main idea, I'd be very interested to learn how you see it manifested.'

'Well, then, I'd like to begin the elaboration of this further aspect of my thinking in what at first sight may seem a rather far-fetched way, in the realm of more personal psychology again.

You know that I'm passionately interested in Arthur Schnitzler. Whenever I want "to go home", I read Schnitzler. This may surprise you since his general reputation, on the basis of his autobiography *Jugend in Wien*, Youth in Vienna, is of being "ein alter Erotiker" – in English one would no doubt say "a dirty old man"! Now he certainly had a weakness for the ladies – there always seemed to be a girl waiting for him in bed, like soup standing in the oven – but as a thinker and writer he went beyond this. The leading academic authority on Schnitzler, Martin Swailes, in his *Arthur Schnitzler*, maintains that he is above all a moralist. Interestingly enough he brings this out in his chapter on the relationship between Schnitzler and Freud. He begins by noting that Freud wrote to Schnitzler fairly late in his life to say that he had avoided meeting him out of a "Doppelgängerscheu", a timidity about meeting his double. Martin Swailes goes on to show very well that for Schnitzler it was, perhaps paradoxically, only fidelity in a relationship and the inevitable self-limitation involved that could bring man true self-fulfilment and this could be undermined and even destroyed by the exploration of those darker urges in man which seemed to be associated with Freud's enterprise. Thus the *Traumnovelle* evokes an absolute orgy of eroticism and yet it ends with the main actor finding his way home to his wife and to the purposeful, peaceful and meaningful life and structure of his family. It was thus for him only the freedom to overcome the tremendously powerful unconscious impulses to sexuality within him that gives meaning to man's life. This is how Martin Swailes puts it:

> There is one particular interesting moment in the Freud and Breuer *Studies*. In the case of Fraulein Elisabeth von R., Freud suggests to the patient that the cause of her pains and hysterical symptoms is her repressed love for her brother-in-law. She is outraged by this and Freud attempts to pacify her by using two arguments:"That we are not responsible for our feelings and that her behaviour, the fact that she had fallen ill in these circumstances, was sufficient evidence of her moral character." Freud here raises two issues – individual responsibilities, and morals- which are for Schnitzler an insistent dilemma, the cause for infinite reflection and questioning. From Freud's prespective they are in no sense problematical. *For Schnitzler, however, man must believe in his own free will and responsibility, in his existence as a moral agent, in order that the business of living should have meaning and value.*[13]

13. at pp.125 and 126. The italics are added.

You see, here again, even in a man who had so fully experienced his impulse-ridden being, we see the affirmation of the possibility and the necessity of going beyond our impulses towards something higher by grasping the innermost core of our freedom.

Now it may be that it was Schnitzler's personal tragedy not to be able to live up to his insights as a dramatist and moralist, but we can see the process he intuited more positively attested by others. There is, for instance, what William James had noted about the utterances of St John of the Cross and St Theresa in his classic *Varieties of Religious Experience*:

> Saint John of the Cross, writing of the *intuitions and "touches"* by which God teaches the substance of the soul, tells us that – "They enrich it marvellously. A single one of them *may be sufficient to abolish at a stroke certain imperfections of which the soul during its whole life had vainly tried to rid itself*, and to leave it adorned with virtues and loaded with supernatural gifts ..."
>
> Saint Teresa is as emphatic, and much more detailed. You may remember a passage I quoted from her in my first lecture. There are many similar pages in her autobiography. Where in literature is a more evidently veracious account of the formation of a new centre of spiritual energy than is given in her description of the effects of certain ecstasies which in departing leave the soul upon a higher level of emotional excitment?
>
> "Often, infirm and wrought upon with dreadful pains before the ecstasy, the soul emerges from it full of health and admirably disposed for action ... as if God had willed that the body itself, already obedient to the soul's desires, should share in the soul's happiness ... For my own part, *I feel as if it would be a remedy for all our ills*."[14]

This, to my mind, is all of a piece with *certain biographical fragments* which have much impressed me.

14. at pp.413-415. The italics are added.

The case of Goethe is well-known. He worked on *Faust* for some sixty years in all, but his most creative period was at the end of his life when he worked on practically nothing else than what he called his *Hauptgeschäft*, the main business, of the second part of Faust, getting up at five o'clock in the morning. He completed the book, sealed the package of his manuscript and within a few months he was dead. It is therefore doubly interesting that Thomas Mann, in his turn, who also died in his eighties, in a Zürich hospital, said to his favourite daughter Erica, on a visit: "If I hadn't started to write *Dr Faustus* ten years ago, I should have died then." Then there's a number of incidents involving cancer. You probably know that Sir Laurence Olivier was told that he had cancer of the prostate gland and would not be able to act again. He was so fired with anger that he fought the illness, rallied and is still with us. Such was his tremendous will to live. Similarly Sir Francis Chichester was also told that he had lung cancer and was expected to die. The story goes that he literally crawled onto his boat. But the incredible happened. In coping with the adventure and in successfully circumnavigating the globe single handed in his boat, he came back after a few months more or less fit. In fact he made the journey a second time, though when he came back the second time he was dying and had to be picked up before quite completing his journey. Then, recently, a woman said on television that she had been told she was suffering from cancer, was given some six months to live, had set out collecting £2,000,000 for a scanner for the detection of early symptoms of cancer – and she recovered! She was asked how she had managed. Her reply was cautious: "Cancer isn't only a physical thing, it's also an emotional thing, above all it's a spiritual thing."

Do you see my point? In simple language, all that orientation towards the future, *being possessed of a sense of the future and so experiencing liberation of the energies of life and healing* – all that this means is having something to live for.'

'I must say that I find these "biographical fragments", as you call them, very striking too, Martin, and I'm particularly interested by the little stories about sufferers from cancer. The thing which most impressed me about the Bristol experience in dealing with cancer which was given wide publicity on television recently is that their little brochure is called "A School for *Living*": they have realised that coping with at least this disease, if not perhaps with all disease, is a matter of the revaluation of one's whole life. By the same token, I'm convinced that a medical friend of mine is on the right track in setting up a pilot research project in London involving three groups: those undergoing merely conventional therapy for cancer, those also having counselling, and those further having an opportunity for training in meditation and visualisation. For this experiment embodies the insight that we have not only a physical but an emotional and a spiritual dimension to our existence. This would again accord with your saying that the essence of the forward drive is the aspiration towards and intimation of a "higher self".'

'Exactly so, Marcus, but there's more to it than even this. The clue to what I want to go on to say is given in a little pamphlet by a certain Reverend Roy McVicar called *Healing through Meditation*. He says, on page 4: "The need for purpose in living to enable one to find personal fulfilment is essential for health, for man is an integral part of the whole evolutionary process which through him is moving forward towards fulfilment. This means that the deep inner purpose of life is this forward movement." You see, so far we have been talking as if the forward drive were only a matter of a process within the person, whereas McVicar is pointing out that this process within the person has to be seen to be part of the cosmic process. I think that this is what the so-called "spontaneous mystical experiences" and the "consciousness explosion" are really about. They are described, for example, in such books as *The Watcher on the Hill* and *Imprisoned Splendour* by Raynor C. Johnson. In the sort of "spontaneous mystical experiences" described by Raynor C. Johnson a man momentarily experiences the splendour of his higher being, released from the prison of his earth-bound body, and he suddenly becomes overwhelmingly aware of the glory of the cosmos. So what seems to be breaking out in more and more people is an awareness of responsibility for the whole earth. It's as if any profound interior transformation of their nature had to be transmitted mysteriously to the material life of the earth. Again I should like to quote you one particular expression of this new awareness from the pen of a certain Hans-Jürgen Baden in a little book called *Wissende, Verschwiegene, Eingeweihte*:

The transformation of base matter into nobler stuff and above all into gold, now takes on a parabolic significance. Redemption too is a matter of man's renewal, of the new creature which bears the divine seal emerging out of the old. Is it therefore a big step for this transformation to be carried over to the very cosmos so that it now becomes alight and alive with the spirit? What else do the images of the new earth and the new heaven prophesied in the New Testament and glimpsed by believers mean than that the mystery of man spreads to the world and includes everything? Nor is the mystery of the depth of matter an obstacle to this process, for matter longs to cast off its heavy character as mere stuff and to change into a resplendent, ethereal medium. The alchemist with his experiments pursues the elevation of matter, so that it becomes transparent and lucid and as gold wins lasting worth. This redemption is not limited to the human realm. Matter is already meant to take a share in this lightness and spiritualisation to which it has a claim in the liberation of the alchemist. Matter presses beyond itself into the no-longer material, it takes on the radiance of the light, the weightlessness of the wind.

It is from these golden, crystal, ethereal elements that the apocalyptic city glimpsed by visionairies is built. That dualism of spirit and matter which is built immoveably into so many theologico-philosophical systems is transcended. Spirit penetrates ever further into matter, into the sheer stuffness of things – and bascially waits to be overcome and illuminated by the former.'[15]

'If I might interrupt you again, Martin, I want to say that I find this way of looking at things very exciting too. For one thing, the bell which your remarks ring for me is the antique notion variously known as the Tao in Chinese culture, Rta in the Hindu culture, natural law in the Western culture, and so evocatively caught in Wordworth's lines composed above Tintern Abbey:

> And I have felt
> A presence that disturbs me with the joy
> Of elevated thought; a sense sublime
> Of something far more deeply interfused,
> Whose dwelling is the light of the setting suns,
> And the round ocean and the living air,
> And the blue sky, and in the mind of man:
> A motion and a spirit, that impels
> All thinking things, all objects of all thought,
> And rolls through all things.

At the same time, what you say imparts to these primordial notions the contemporary feel for evolution, for ecology, for global inter-dependence and solidarity, and for the fulfilment of man's destiny on earth.'

'Yes, indeed, Marcus, and perhaps you'll see better how I've come to the notion of what I hope it's not too grandiloquent to call the eschatology of counselling – an awareness that people can and need to awaken into a responsibility for the "fate of the earth", to use the title of a recent best-seller by Jonathan Schell.'

'Could one then say that counselling nowadays can include as it were an initiation into the forward movement and destiny of planet earth itself, into the creative process of the cosmos –

15. at pp.100 and 101.

which we were really beginning to say last time, but are now saying in a fuller way?'

'That would be my meaning, yes, Marcus.'

'And if we're agreed on that, can we not add one more thing?

You've stressed, and rightly, that all this requires strenuous and unremitting effort, that even what you call the raising of the sluice-gate or the removal of obstacles requires such effort. At the same time what results from this effort is an insertion or integration or subordination of the individual ego into something greater then the ego, a cause, what Esther Harding calls a "suprapersonal value", what people have traditionally called God. It's as if the innermost truth of man is that he opens out into something beyond and greater than himself and on which he depends, as if the real end of his self-actualisation is, as Victor Frankl has pointed out very incisively in an essay entitled "Beyond Self-actualisation and Self-expression",[16] his self-surmounting, self-transcendence. It's as if what you have called the "higher self" consists in being united to the Other. This is once again the truth at the bottom of the well, the individual wellspring's very reservoir. But this surely means that what has hitherto been experienced as effort, strenuous effort, *tapas*, energy, is felt more and more as a surender to this greater force or power or person – Life or Love or Truth itself. In that respect, therefore, one is passive. This is brought out in a very beautiful passage from Thomas Merton:

> At the centre of our being is a point of nothingness which is untouched by sin and by illusion, a point of pure truth, a point or spark which belongs entirely to God, which is never at our disposal, from which God disposes of our lives, which is inaccessible to the fantasies of our own mind or the brutalities of our own will. This little point of nothingness and of *absolute poverty* is the pure glory of God in us. It is so to speak his name written in us, as our

16. *Psychotherapy and Existentialism* (1973), at pp.45 ff.

poverty, as our indigence, as our dependence, as our sonship. It is like a pure diamond, blazing with the invisible light of heaven. It is in everybody ... The gate of heaven is everywhere.'

'Yet this element of self-surrender – which would, I suppose, be called the receiving of grace? –presupposes a preliminary effort of strict discipline, the effort of making oneself a vessel which can receive grace, so that the effort of the self is a first stage. Don't you agree, Marcus?'

'I wouldn't put it quite like that. It's very difficult to talk about. I don't wish to say myself that at any stage there is unalloyed, unqualified self-effort to be then followed by grace. I believe that grace – God – is active all the time in the life of the individual and of the race, so that we have to find a way of talking about what goes on which does justice to both elements – the effort and the grace, the active and the passive – all the time. So I should prefer to talk in terms of the different phases of subjective experience. For me God is working in us and to that extent we are passive all the time, though in the initial phases we experience our active side of it, and it is only in subsequent phases that we have a more felt sense of the passivity which has nevertheless been present all the time. Any description in terms of effort and grace, activity and passivity, is a description of alternations of first one, then the other within us from our point of view. Something like that. Do you agree?'

'I do, and yet we do also have to allow for the fact that we can, for example, get drunk or become involved in a passionate infatuation which damages and almost destroys us, so that God will have difficulty in working with us all the time. So in that sense this basic discipline, the rule of life, is applicable.'

'I must agree with that. I don't disagree with the facts, only with the description of the facts. I'm just trying to do justice to the presence of both God's working and our effort all the time

17. *Conjectures of a Guilty Bystander* (1968), at p.158.

and so hit off the relationship between them. I should still want to say that our working is in the last analysis our co-working with God, that any discipline we may develop is a discipline precisely of becoming more and more congruent with God, so that any activity of ours is passive in relation to his initiative, but I should also have to say that the degree of God's working in us is a matter of what we allow, so that, paradoxically our effort is the measure of our becoming passive to God.'

'With that I can completely agree, Marcus.'

'Well, then, can we go one step further yet, Martin? Even if we can agree that the strenuous effort of moving into the future turns out of be a matter of the self-surrendering integration into the force of the future made present now, we have to acknowledge that it will always be only partial and liable to interruption, if only the interruption of personal death. But isn't this where the, say, Hindu notion of *jivan-mukti*, emancipation while still alive, as M. Hiriyanna puts it,[18] or the Christian notion of grace as the germ of glory, *semen gloriae*, finds its completion in the Judaeo-Christian intuition of the resurrection of the body: the new life of the future is inaugurated and anticipated now, but in such a way that it will be resumed and completed beyond any interruption?'

'I can again completely agree with that, Marcus. For me, since the Christ event there can be a "christing" of the personality which consists in the influx of supersensible life, light and love that gradually transforms the total personality in almost imperceptible stages, and such occasionally occurring phenomena as weightlessness, the odour of sanctity, the incorruptibility of the body are pointers to the final resurrection of the body. We have come back in our own way to St John's notion of "the new heaven and the new earth".

All this is, however, rather lofty. We may be over-reaching ourselves. I'd like to come back to earth. What sums up a good deal of what I've been saying today is something more homely,

18. *Outlines of Indian Philosophy* (1932), at p.19.

at least it is so for me since it is taken from the world of music which is so important for me. There's a little book about Mozart's "Die Zauberflöte" by Alfons Rosenberg and in it he first quotes Ludwig Börne's telling words about Mozart and then adds his own comment:

"... Mozart's music reflects back everyone's own and present feelings like a mirror, but somewhat ennobled; we recognise in it the poetry of existence". In other words, ever since Mozart's time men have in his music recognised their true condition and state cleared of everything that can tarnish it from without, the sensual man recognises himself as the godlike man he has been called to be by nature.[19]

That's the release of the drive towards the future in counselling in a nutshell.'

'I'm very content to end on this note today, Martin. Thank you.'

19. (1972), at p.8.

Dialogue 3:
Personality and
Power

Go, release them, Ariel.
My charms I'll break, their senses I'll restore
And they shall be themselves ...

The charm dissolves apace;
And as the morning steals upon the night,
Melting the darkness, so their rising senses
Begin to chase the ignorant fumes that mantle
Their clearer reason ...

Shakespeare *The Tempest* Act V, Scene 1

'I'd like to take up a question today which is implicit in many
of our previous discussions, Martin. You've often said or
suggested that the counsellor's personality plays a very
important part in the development of the client. It is a fact of
therapy, as it is of life, that one person may indeed influence
another enormously. But this immediately raises the question
whether the counsellor does not, or may not, exercise undue
influence on the client, more or less crudely impose himself,
manipulate, violate the other, and this is really an ethical
question. There are, therefore, two questions here: Does the
counsellor exercise power? And, if so, how is he to exercise it
in the client's interests rather than against them?

Now I'd like to take the first question first: Does the
counsellor exercise power?'

'I think that he undoubtedly does, Marcus. This is implicit
in my conviction, to which you've already referred, that the

personality of the counsellor, what he is, quite apart from anything he does or says, can of itself be of decisive importance for the client. What we and other people discuss in terms of listening, exploring and guiding, enabling, encouraging and eliciting and so on, is the counsellor *in action*; but what I've come to realise more and more is that something can happen between people even before a gesture is made or a word is spoken. We've talked before about the mystery of the *Gespräch*, the dialogue; I now think we also need to take account of something we've not yet talked about, the mystery of the *Begegnung*, the encounter – the sheer meeting, the event of two entities, two entelechies coming into contact and communication. This is a mysterious happening in which the client takes in, certainly with a sensible but almost with a degree of supersensible perception, say, the very personality of the counsellor. What is for me a wonderful and an almost archetypal illustration of this is given in *Twentieth Century Mystics and Sages* by Anne Bancroft, who had spent her childhood in the Quaker village of Jordans in Buckinghamshire before becoming a mother of four children and finally a lecturer and researcher in comparative religion. The saint or guru in question here is Ramani Maharshi who died in 1950. The book contains a photograph of him and it's important to see his face, it's important to see his eyes, because much of the mystery of the *Begegnung*, encounter, happens by virtue of seeing, gazing, rather than through talking. People came to him from all over the world, and he just sat there. Here is a description of the typical scene of the daily *darshan*, or audience, by a Buddhist monk who came to visit the ashram:

By the time we arrived the Maharshi was generally established in his usual place on the couch at the far end of the hall, where he would either recline against a bolster or, though more rarely, sit up cross-legged. Sometimes we arrived early enough to hear the chanting of the Vedas by a group of Tamil brahmins, with which the morning darshan began ... After the chanting was over, and the brahmins had filed out of the hall, not much seemed to happen. The Maharshi sat on his couch. From time to time someone would approach him with a question or a request, would receive a brief reply, sometimes no more than a look or a gesture, and would then return to his place. That was all. The rest of the time the sixty or seventy people sitting in the hall either simply looked at the Maharshi, which was what the word *darshan* literally meant, or else closed their eyes and meditated. Talking was by no means prohibited, and muted greetings would sometimes be exchanged between new arrivals and friends in the congregation, but for the most part the devotees sat quiet and motionless, hour after hour and a great silence reigned in the hall. One could not sit there for long without becoming aware that this silence was not mere absence of sound but a positive spiritual influence, even a spiritual force. It was as though a stream flowed through it, a stream of purity, and this breeze, this stream, seemed to emanate from the silent nodding figure on the couch, who did nothing in particular, only reading the letters that were brought to him or glancing, every now and then, at some member of the congregation with keen but kindly eyes. Sitting there in the hall ... I felt the stream flow over me, felt it flow over body and mind, over thoughts and emotions, until body, mind, thoughts and emotions had all been washed away, and there remained nothing but a great shining peace.[1]

Do you see: this is a heightened instance of what can go on between people even before and without words, it brings out the immense healing effects of coming into the mere presence of such a personality and any peace and spontaneity he may have attained. In this connection, I remember too how Steiner once visited a woman with a small handicapped child and said: "Es ist der Mensch der heilt" – "It's the human being who

1. at p.157.

heals". So it's not only what the counsellor says or even knows which heals but above all what he *is*, the silent stream of his being and presence to the other. I firmly believe this, and of course, it emphasises for me the importance of preparation. Without it one is in danger or remaining one's ordinary self, and the time of preparation is at least an attempt to transcend this condition in the direction of being more open and peaceful.'

'I appreciate your distinction between the mystery of the *Gespräch*, the dialogue, and the mystery of the *Begegnung*, the meeting, Martin. I find your illustration enlightening. But in another sense what you say reinforces my difficulty. I'm as convinced as you are that what goes on between two people can be so subtle and full that it's ultimately ineffable, unanalysable, and can be referred to only by some such word as mystery or alchemy. At the same time, it's part of my bent – which will by now be familiar and perhaps even maddening to you! – to want nevertheless to try to make what is ineffable as articulate as possible, to reclaim for speech as much as possible of the mysterious. So while we have to recognise the limits of what can be said, we all have to try to push these limits back. We can and must talk about the mystery, and yet I persist in wanting to ask whether we can say anything more about it.'

'I think we can, and I should like to mention a few facts which have struck me as particularly significant in regard to this mystery of *Begegnung*, meeting. Moreover these facts are factors of ordinary life since a meeting of the order of a *Begegnung* can, of course, take place there, so meeting in the context of counselling is once again only a heightened instance of essentially the same event. In life, then, people can gaze at each other and suddenly have the feeling – rightly or wrongly, but often enough rightly – that they have *found* each other. Meeting and gazing are also the mystery of finding. In this connection, I should like to mention a few examples.

You may well know that Sir William Walton, the composer, had many love affairs in his earlier life, then went to Ischia to deliver a lecture. The hall was full, and at the very edge of the crowded hall a girl was standing, an Argentinian girl. After the lecture Sir William Walton was asked how he liked their girls. He said: "You see that girl" – pointing to the Argentinian girl – "I'm going to marry her." She was overwhelmed, and thought he was mad. Within a few days he had convinced her that there was every reason to get married. They did, and they had a very happy marriage for thirty years. The mystery of gazing and finding. Similarly, Bruno Walter, the conductor, was on a ship, saw a girl, not particularly attractive, looked at her and said: "That's the girl I'm going to marry." Then old Martin Gregory himself, you know, when he was young, stood in a certain place, which he still remembers to this very day, and a girl who went to school with him spoke to him about another girl called Emma Vogel. He heard bells ringing and had the feeling that this was the girl he had been waiting for. It was.'

'You hadn't then even seen her?'

'No, I hadn't. I saw her later. Be that as it may, what is to me one of the most beautiful illustrations of the meeting which takes place in the depths of two people's being when they gaze at each other is taken from the life of Alban Berg – you know, Berg of the new Viennese school, the pupil of Schönberg, composer of *Wozzek* and modern atonal music. I'd like to show you two photos of Alban and Helene Berg, but before I do that I'll tell you the story attached to their meeting. Alban is an unusual name, even in German, but it so happened that Helene as a little girl loved fairy stories, as young children do, and her particular favourite was a story about a prince called Alban. Then, in later life, she met Alban Berg, they saw each other, gazed at each other and soon married. Here are two photographs of them looking at each other after their marriage. I think you'll agree that these pictures also bear out Hugo von Hofmannsthal's saying that the most intimate encounter is not the sexual one but the encounter of gazing into each other's eyes.

Now what I think takes place in such cases is not only gazing but an element of predestined finding, something in the nature of *karma*. In other words, there is, for some reason you can analyse as you wish, an expectation or foreknowledge of somebody one wants and hopes to find, it may be a spouse, or a lover, or a doctor. People do say to a doctor: "You're the man I've been looking for." They can even say: "I feel I've known you for a long time." As I say, you can explain this as you will, in terms of reincarnation or whatever. All I can say for myself is that when I had started to know Emma I had one of the three big dreams of my life, in which I dreamed that I had waited five hundred and forty years to come to earth in order to meet her and to be there when she was here – and we were born and grew up within a mile of each other, across the little Danube canal. So for me part of the mystery of meeting and gazing is a deep undercurrent of personal destiny, a sense of finding or recognising somebody who belongs to you, who has been sent to you. When I look at a picture like that of Alban Berg I get the feeling that, unconsciously of course, they experience something that goes far beyond the ordinary perception of seeing each other, they recognise something which has been dormant or been buried in the abyss of time and which they discover – or recover.'

'These stories are truly remarkable, Martin. You have conveyed very clearly what you mean by the power and influence which can emanate silently from a person in what you call the mystery of the *Begegnung*, the encounter. I take it that for you this is the product not just of the immediate preparation for any particular meeting but of the preparation and discipline of a whole life. But this very fact brings us up against the second problem I indicated at the beginning, namely, how this power is to be exercised in the client's favour and not to his detriment. How is the power not to be manipulative but freeing? How is the client to avoid just joining the circle of the counsellor's admirers and followers – almost the charmed circle, because a person with a strong personality can keep another in thrall as if by a spell? Would you say that the way a counsellor can as it were return the client to himself is above all by dealing with, working through the "transference", to use a term taken from psychoanalytic practice and theory?'

'Yes and no, but perhaps you could first of all say a little more explicitly what you mean by "transference"?'

'Well, the topic is very well explained in the chapter of that title in the excellent summary of the Freudian tradition, *The Patient and the Analyst*, by J. Sandler, C. Dare and A. Holder. But I'll try to explain what I understand by this term in my own words. By tranference, then, I understand the realisation of that tendency in us all to see and feel the new in the light of the old, the present in terms of the past, the tendency to assimilate what is offered us fresh now to what we have already experienced; therefore to see people in the present as if they were figures from the past, especially very significant figures,and so to relive the loves, hates, reactions and overreactions, dependencies etc. of the past here and now. Now this is a universal human tendency but it manifests itself more intensely and systematically in intimate relationships, and therefore in the therapeutic relationship. The intense form of this universal tendency in love and in therapy is well brought out by Monica Furlong in a book which is full of insights, *Travelling In*:

> "Into a transference a person will bring all his relationships". This was written by an analyst about the analytical situation, but it is equally true of the transference of the person in love … The years which the locust hath eaten are restored. The pain of the old relationship with father and mother is relived, and we are born again, by the charity and the wisdom of the lover. A dual task is forced upon the lover, and acted out, sometimes in disguise, sometimes consciously; the infant returns again to the womb, to his mother's arms, to the breast, and is healed. To set off once again upon the journey.[2]

I hope that this is a clear enough indication of what I

2. at p.32.

understand by transference. If so, I wonder whether you believe in transference and whether you deal with it?'

'Your indication, as you call it, is indeed very clear, and I recognise fully that what you have referred to in this way occurs in life and in therapy. Even if you are not an analyst, a patient will tend to *adopt* you in a certain role. Now my experience is that by and large a client had a need to do this. He doesn't do this because he's nasty or possessive – that he may be too – but because he has, for example, been deprived of a father or because, in the case of a woman, she has a very ineffectual husband or has no lover and has no one to turn to for guidance and care. So, speaking for myself, I long accepted it as inevitable that, to begin with, a client claims me in a certain role. The question is, what to do about it. This is a very subtle matter, and can be very delicate where, for example, it's as a lover that a woman wants to claim you. There's a little story which contains my response in a nutshell. I don't know whether you ever saw the film *Funny Face*, with Audrey Hepburn?'

'No I didn't.'

'Well, in it Audrey Hepburn played the part of a woman to whom a philosopher makes amorous advances and she said: "I thought you were a philosopher, you're just a man." In other words, the moment the therapist yields to the temptation of letting himself act in the role which the client wants, whether as father or as lover ...'

'By way of "counter-transference"?'

'Yes, this is counter-transference – then he's lost. But my point is that if I first accept the client's doing this as the expression of a need, then my reaction is to sit it out. I wait. I let the onslaught, as it were, go over me, if need be for a considerable time. I try not to reject the client's need and the fact of what he's doing. I think that this would be a mistake. I try to accept it within myself but I transform, transfigure it. So if I'm being asked to be, for instance, a father, then I begin, not by allowing myself to be cast in this role, but by accepting this potentiality of fatherhood in me out of my total humanity, *als Mensch*, as man.

This, however, is only a beginning, and what needs in principle to follow is again summed up for me in an experience of the whole process which I had when I still didn't understand it. I was seeing a woman, still a friend of the family, who had been deprived of good parents, had a completely unfulfilled marriage, and had no friend. She adopted me as a father figure and was desperate to adopt me as a lover. She was sometimes so disturbed that she couldn't open her month – because she is a very passionate woman. She wrote the most extravagant erotic poetry. But because I sat it out, she began to respect me as a human being who cared for her and could guide her. The point is that the energies released through the transference – and where loving and being loved are concerned, these are enormous – became transformed, redirected, rechannelled, in this case into studying, going to a teachers' training college, making an excellent career of teaching, in other words building her life. If she hadn't released her energies through the very emotional storm, and if I had tried to stifle this, which I didn't, she wouldn't have got on. So the transference, as you call it, is something which has to be welcomed and then rechannelled and transformed.'

'That makes very good sense, Martin. What you're saying is that, at least now, you recognise the phenomenon of transference.'

'Yes.'

'And the possibility of counter-transference as a trap?'

'Absolutely as a trap.'

'But the way you deal with it is subtly different from the psychoanalytic way of dealing with it. For whereas in the latter tradition the analyst deals with the transference by "interpreting" it (albeit "on the basis" of his "refusal to act in the role in which he is cast", as Sadler, Dare and Holder put it in a footnote[3]), you take the transference very seriously and sympathetically but in order to let it be transformed from

3. at p.42.

within, and on the basis of an active awareness of the client's general human qualities and strengths.'

'No, I don't comment on the way the client acts towards me in one role or another. For instance, if I'd made a comment on the case of the woman I referred to, an explosion would have taken place. But I recognise the need and the character of what's going on and try to integrate and humanise it.'

'In this respect I think you're nearer to Jung. For although the Freudians have begun to take more explicit theoretical or official notice of the "human dimension in psychoanalytical practice", to quote the title of a recent book, Jung never, I think, attached so much importance to the transference, preferring to encourage the client's native and generally human resources, rather as you seem to do in your own way.'

'Yes, for me the whole exchange is and must remain a profoundly human experience. I must live through it and work through the relationship and the trust. This is not something which happens automatically. I often say that, when a client comes in, I can so to speak smell whether he or she will relate to me. But if you for your part try to meet the other in a friendly way as a human being, without preconceived ideas, inhibitions or aversions – which takes a great deal of work – then the transference and the rechannelling of energies has a chance to take place.'

'I think you've given me a very complete account of how you deal with the reality behind the term transference. For you, then, transference is an opportunity to enable the client to release and realise his own innate energies, and since the basic problem we're dealing with is how the undoubted power of the therapist is to be made to serve the client rather than himself, this is a valuable contribution to seeing how this actually works.

Characteristically, however, I still feel that we haven't pushed the investigation of how the therapist's power communicates and deposits itself in the client as his, the client's, power, quite far enough. You've spoken about the coming to head and the redirecting of energies as if the process were a sort of discharge outwards and then a reflux back to the client, so that they are now available to his own purposes. But what are these purposes? And has the intervention of the counsellor and his personality and power anything to do with this further process? Put another way, your approach seems to consist in accepting the other's need for a father figure, or lover, whatever, into yourself, allowing it to resonate there with the corresponding possibilities within yourself, but, by retaining your own identity and purpose and so gently pushing the energy back to the client, encouraging it to move beyond where it was, according to its own dynamic. So, my question is: Do you think that the energies experienced in the transference do have an inner dynamic, and, if so, what? You seem to believe in something very much like what Winnicott in *Playing and Reality* called "the natural evolution of the transference"[4], and so my question is also: Do you think that there is some inner direction to such a "natural evolution", and, if so, what is it? Does anything more go on between counsellor and client than we have already seen?'

'I do indeed think that there is a dynamic, as you put it, and that it does have an inner direction, just as I also think that a lot more goes on between counsellor and client to help this forward, and here I must first repeat that putting another in the position of father, lover, whatever, is something which happens in ordinary life too, so that it's the expression of a human need deeply implanted in human nature and carried into the therapeutic situation. But there is more to it than such a human need to find a father, lover, etc. What *is* more, to put it in an extreme form, is the need, conscious or half-conscious, to search for the *true image of man*, something which transcends the ordinary frailties of human nature, something which has about it a sense of permanence, immortality. And in this connection, I should like to quote two wonderful lines from one of the less well known poems of Rilke, *Winterliche Stanzen*:

4. at p.101.

Los ohne gleichen: im Vergehn zu sein:
Zu schweben unter lauten Stellen Schwindens –

Fate like no other: dying yet to be, to be poised in a world of dwindling places. You see, for Rilke, the destiny and fate of man is like that of no other – to overcome, transcend ageing, mortality; dying yet to be, to lift himself up to and remain soaring or poised, *schweben*, in a sphere which is durable. This is what the philosopher, the sage, the priest, the saint, represent. People feel that here is a being who has not been tarnished, corrupted by the inevitable ravages of mortality; although sick, ageing, frail, he still shares a destiny like no other. So when we do go on to ask what it is more precisely that people want their energies for, I suggest that they are looking for the true image of man. This is surely to say in effect that they're searching for the essence of the religious.'

'Because the true image of man is then seen to include the fact that he somehow derives his being from God? Because the depths or heights of man are in the last analysis seen to consist in his dependence on God?'

'Precisely, Marcus, and in this connection I'm also convinced that Prabhavananda and Isherwood are right when they say in their commentary on the Gītā: "True religion is not taught but transmitted like light."[5] So people are looking for this light, and once they see it they feel that they've found what they'd been looking for.'

'I see what you're getting at, Martin. But isn't there an ambiguity in the way you're putting your point which needs clearing up? You say that what people are secretly looking for, beyond the figures of people they've missed, like a father or a lover, is the true image of man, which, when met, is like a light from a transcendent source and is therefore something religious in character, in so far as it seems to be a participation in the divine. You say further that the counsellor can convey this true image of man as made in the likeness of God in so far as he shares in something of the religious quality of the

5. *How to Know God*, at p.150.

philosopher, sage, priest or saint. But are you saying that clients are searching for the true image of God as located in another human being, including the counsellor, or are they searching for it as something for and in themselves? In other words, is the other, including the counsellor, the object of the search for the imagehood of God or only the occasion? Must the other, including the counsellor, actually bear the image of God or can he somehow suggest and evoke it even despite any relative personal inadequacy, being perhaps an only too earthen vessel who nevertheless bears treasure which is not his own?'

'That's a very important distinction, Marcus, and it bears directly on the office of the counsellor and the raison d'etre of the relationship with the client. For it is precisely to the extent that a client's need becomes manifest as a need to find the true image of man that he's in danger of locating this in the counsellor and *not* making it his own, and the counsellor is correspondingly exposed to one of the most insidious traps. For the more spiritualised a person becomes, the more attractive but thereby also the more powerful he becomes in relation to his client. Once again Prabhavananda and Isherwood put this very clearly in their commentary on the Gītā *How to Know God*:

Up to a certain point, temptation increases with spiritual growth. As the spiritual aspirant ceases to be a mere beginner and gains some mystical experience, his personality becomes magnetic. He finds that he can exert psychological power over others, and also sexual attraction. At the same time, his senses grow keener and more capable of enjoyment. It is therefore easy for him to become involved in power- and sex-relationships which will make him forget his original purpose. The very people who are drawn to him because of the god-like quality they see in his nature may be the ones who are most responsible for his gradual alienation from God.[6]

6. at p.198.

'So you seem to be saying in effect that the counsellor can indeed have great power, in fact that he gains in power in proportion to his spiritualisation, and that he has to make a conscious effort and choice as it were to return that power back to the client rather than to take it to himself?'

'Yes, that's what I'm implying.'

'Well, if that's so, then I think that I begin to see the solution to the problem I put at the beginning, namely, how the undoubted power of the therapist is not to be abused. The answer, it now seems to me, is, to put it briefly, that power needs to become more and more *shared*.

It's simple enough to state this conclusion. It's not so easy to convey how I've come to it. I ask you to bear with me as I try to explain my view.

The germ of the idea as to how power comes to be shared in the *Gespräch*, the dialogue, between counsellor and client had been sown in me, as I now realise, in a reading of *Introduction to Psychotherpay* by D. Brown and J. Pedder. For I had been struck by the way in which, at various points in this book, they referred to the gathering process of exchange between therapist and client in terms of a "culture" or language. In this they seemed to have been influenced by the conception of what goes on between the ordinary medical doctor and the patient developed by Balint. By "culture" they thus mean a way of talking, a way of looking at and dealing with things, a language and a "form of life" gradually developed and built up between therapist and client, at first largely under the leadership of the doctor or therapist but then gradually on a more equal basis.

Now this idea of what goes on between therapist and client is interesting enough in its own right. It becomes more inward when we follow the reference at least implicitly made here in the use of this term "culture" and trace it back to the work of the later Donald Winnicott and in particular to the way in which he uncovered the inner essence of the actual process of the making of a culture. For not the least of the discoveries which the later Winnicott made was that the making of a culture even in the larger social sense of the word and therefore also in a narrower bi-personal sense originates and is foreshadowed in the first exchanges between mother and child.

As I understand the inner force of Winnicott's thinking, as deposited in his last book so evocatively called *Playing and Reality*, he was gradually led by his persistent attention to the facts presented by his patients to break through his previous notions and so to become aware of a decisive change in the character of the relationship of a mother and her infant in the normal process of the growth of that relationship. He couched his successive discoveries in terms that have become almost technical: "transitional objects", and "intermediate area" between mother and child and between "subjectivity and objective observation", the "overlap" of personal space between the two, and the development of the capacity for ever more mutual play. But the essential realisation, it seems to me, was about the change from *mere gratification* on the infant's part to the first possibilities of the sort of cooperation he called *play* – and well called play, I think, because exclusive concern with gratification is a form of compulsion, so that moving beyond this creates a freedom in which the infant can begin to be concerned ever more disinterestedly in the other as other, and it is just such freedom that is associated with the term "play". So it was in this form of cooperation that he began to see the genesis and precursor of the making of culture in the larger social sense of that word.

The relevance of all this for us, it seems to me, is this: The developing relationship between the therapist and the client can be seen as an adult recapitulation of the process between mother and child. As Brown and Pedder put it very succinctly: "The transitional object is a joint action of infant and mother; successful therapy is a joint creation of patient and therapist."[7] But the making of culture in this sense is *also* a process of *the gradual relinquishing and divesting of power by the*

7. at p.112.

powerful figure – the mother in the one case, the therapist in the other – and a process of divesting in the direction of an ever greater sharing, until the client is freed of compulsive ties, childish dependencies and such like spells, and so is in a position to form genuinely equal and reciprocal relationships with other adults.

My essential point, therefore, is that the later work of Winnicott is a way of enabling us to see how the initial inequality of power tends to develop towards mutual freedom and therefore towards equalisation of power. The fact that Winnicott thought of himself as explaining the origin not so much of the process that goes on between therapist and client as of culture in its ordinary, and therefore more largely social sense, is not immediately relevant to our larger theme. For if culture, in its larger sense, can now be seen as the macro-social working out of what Winnicott had come to see unfolding at the micro-social level in the relationship of mother and child, then the *Gespräch*, in the sense of a dialogue between two adults, can be seen to stand half-way between the genetic form of the cooperative making of a common language and culture first established between mother and child and the greater social form of the making of culture, such as is described and analysed by, for example, Raymond Williams in his *Culture and Society, 1780-1950*. But this means that we're back to one of your master-insights, namely, that the relationship of therapist and client is only the crystallisation or paradigm of a more general process – in this case the process of conversing and arguing, of pitting and redistributing power which we call culture.'

'Once again, Marcus, you've rather left me behind in your elaboration of my more homely meaning, but I do understand and respond with enthusiasm to your return to my intuition – my "master-insight", as you are pleased to put it – that the *Gespräch* expresses an archetype and that this is why it is what you call a "paradigm".'

'Yes, Martin, I admit that I tend to be drawn into these analyses. I should, however, like to bring them at least a little nearer to more common ways of seeing things by suggesting finally that what I have been trying to analyse in terms of the process of making a culture is the inner explanation of a series of phrases which occur in ordinary speech. I refer to the term "world", in the way in which we say, for example, that we have a "world-view", a *Weltanschauung*, that so-and-so lives in a "world of his own", or that two people don't live in the "same world". Could we not say that the process of counselling, like the process of any true human conversation, of which, as you say, it is the crystallisation, consists in the counsellor learning to live in the world of the client – entering wholly into it, with his feelings as well as with his thought: this would then be the famous "seeing with the other's eyes", getting into his skin – and yet *not relinquishing his own world*, in such a way that the client can in his turn also come to share in the counsellor's world and they can thus progressively come to have at least an over-lapping and inter-mingling, if not an entirely shared world? Isn't this one of the ways of unpacking and understanding those haunting words of Herakleitos which T.S. Eliot placed as the motto of *Four Quartets*:

τοῦ λόγου δ'ἐόντος ξυνοῦ ζώουσιν οἱ πολλοί
ὡς ἰδίαν ἔχοντες φρόνησιν.

which I translate as follows: "There is a shared world and it makes sense as such, but most people live as though they had only a private understanding".

To put it in yet another, and, because more poetically, in a simpler and more universal way, isn't it a matter of what Antoine de St Exupéry said to the effect that love is not so much looking at each other as looking together in the same direction?'

'With that, Marcus, I can whole-heartedly agree. I'm very happy to let you finish our exploration of the theme of the therapist's power with a quotation from a writer in the way you let me finish last time with the evocation of a musician!'

'Thank you very much, Martin.'

Dialogue 4:
Growth and Morality

Ein guter Mensch in seinem dunklen Drange
Ist sich des rechten Weges wohl bewusst.
(Even when in the grip of some dark force, a good man
remains aware of the right way.)

Goethe *Faust*

There is some soul of goodness in things evil
Would men observingly distil it out.

Shakespeare *Henry V* Act IV, Scene 1

'The subject I'd like to discuss with you today, Martin, is
again one we have touched on before, that of growth and
morality. By this I mean the conflict there can be between the
demands of personal growth and the demands of a social code.
The issue can be summed up very simply by an anecdote I
seem to remember you telling me. It concerned a man who
had always had a most unsatisfactory relationship with his wife
but who decided to stay with her and could do so only because
once a year he renewed acquaintance with a woman with
whom he had a very deep rapport at every level, including the
sexual one. Here, then, was a man who could survive and keep
his vitality and even, in a sense, a basic fidelity to his wife only
through infringing common social morality.

Put in a more general way, I again see the problem in terms
of a tension.

On the other hand, it must surely be a critical principle of
counselling that we start with people from where they are and
as they are, and thus as variously flawed and wounded,
suffering from "ungelebtes Leben", unlived life, unfinished

business. We aim to help them move forward but from where they can really move, to facilitate their growth but from what their real growth-points are. But it may be a violation of this need to grow from where they are to expect immediate and complete compliance with a code of morality which is beyond at least their present strength. And this way of understanding the function of counselling is reinforced if we take the developmental view of human beings, the view that we come to our full stature and self-realisation through a *series of stages*, the skipping or only partial working through of which leaves tasks that have to be attended to at some time if the whole process of growth is not to be jeopardised. From this point of view conforming with a code of morality can seem to be an imposition from without, an inhibition of true growth from within. It is as if codes of morality were for mature adults whereas the client is, in some respects, deep down a child or even an infant.

On the other hand, the essence of any code of law and morality, and certainly in the Judaeo-Christian view as reformulated by, for instance, St Thomas Aquinas, is that it is ideally, in principle, educative, that it constitutes a schooling precisely to educe growth, the formed out of the unformed, and, what is more, that it is the eliciting from without of what is within, according to the true dynamism and nature of the individual. Law in principle fits the individual as a glove fits the hand. This is why in the Judaeo-Christian tradition, as I understand it, the law can be made the object of praise and celebration, as in Psalm 119; it is *cantabile*, something to sing about. It is also the reason why for St Thomas Aquinas one of the master images of growing in faith is learning from a wise and kindly "doctor", teacher, who seems to know us better than we know ourselves. In this connection there is a recurrence of the essential idea involved in a most unexpected place. R.D. Laing, in his earlier work, *The Divided Self*, is talking about a schizophrenic girl who "was unable to sustain real autonomy because all she could be vis-a-vis her parents was a compliant thing". He then goes on as follows:

> Even when she began to "be herself", she could at first
> only dare to do so by completely mirroring the doctor's
> reality. She could do this, however, since although his
> reality (his wishes for her) were still another they were
> not alien to her. They were congruent with her own
> authentic desire to be herself.[1]

Do you see: this beautiful phrase, "congruent with her own
authentic desire to be herself", exactly hits off the function of
any code of morality in relation to the individual dynamic to
growth. A system of law is thought of as a complement to, a
drawing out of and a stimulus to growth, *not* its contradiction
and thwarting.

Here, then, is the tension or dilemma. It is interestingly
reinforced by the fact that you are a counsellor and I am a
priest in so far as the counsellor in general estimation, I
suppose, stands for the concept of growth, subjective need,
whereas the priest stands more for the concept of law and
morality, objective demand. The tension I have described is,
therefore, embodied and even polarised between us two. I
should, however, add that I do feel this tension within myself,
in that I am somehow caught, even when wearing my priest's
hat, between encouraging growth even in the face of a code of
morality and commending a code of morality as a challenge to
growth. This, however, is a refinement of the essential tension
I want to indicate. I hope you follow.'

'I follow very well indeed, Marcus, and once again you have
indicated very clearly the quick of a very real problem of life
and counselling. I also completely understand your exposition
of the problem in both its anecdotal and its more generalised
form. You will, however, not be surprised if I say that I prefer
the anecdotal form, since all my thinking, as you know very
well by now, has always started from concrete instances and
cases and always tends to go back to them – it is case-based. At
the same time I don't as a matter of fact remember the
particular story you attribute to me, and for that reason alone

1. at p.173.

I'd like to start with another story, a true story, which illustrates more aspects of the problem. It highlights the hazzards of the dilemma facing anybody alive in our present age in which the individual has to free himself from the ties to collective society in order to find his own path.

As you may remember, I know a man who is now a prominent businessman. He was a very clever boy at school, but most unattractive – no girl ever looked at him. He was in his youth completely deprived of appreciation by girls, so that he was unfulfilled in this respect. It was therefore almost predictable that with his tempestuous disposition he would reach out, storm towards some solution sooner or later. Well, he became a tycoon and married a woman older than himself. The marriage was never very exciting, but he had many sexual relationships with women on his staff. His sexual relationships were thus for the most part episodic but he also had long-standing relationships outside business. Nevertheless he remained unfulfilled. I didn't hear from him for a long time, then had a letter which revealed a personal situation which to me was quite astonishing. He had met a woman who was twenty years younger than himself – a woman of fifty can still be very fresh! He had settled down to living with her in the city from Monday to Friday, as it were his working week, and returning at weekends to live with his wife in their country house. She had been loyal to him, supported him and had given him four or five children. So he had two women.'

'A wife at home and a mistress in the city. A classic case. Did his wife know about his other life?'

'He was very careful not to reveal too many details but it was clear that she knew his situation in general and I've no doubt that she had accepted it. Now the interesting thing is that he not only lives with his mistress in the city but every year takes her on world tours, leaving his wife at home. He said that, even before establishing this relationship, he had fairly strong feelings of guilt and there's no doubt that his wife suffers, to put it mildly. So, here is a man who has followed his own law and realised his unfulfilled eros and his own inner growth but he did so by breaking with a morality which was not here imposed from without since nobody bothered with his private life but which was a matter of ordinary human consideration.'

'Yes, this story does illustrate the conflict and all the more so because you state that this man felt guilty and that his wife suffered. I suspect that the fact of guilt in even so apparently a liberated man tells us something important. But I'm certainly concerned about the hurt and grief on the part of the wife. What is the validity of a so-called law of inner growth which inevitably results in one or more others being so hurt?'

'Of course, that concerns me too, Marcus. I'm saying, however, in the first place that one has duties to others but also duties to oneself, to life itself and that one therefore has to take on the responsibility of being a lawgiver to oneself, even though harm to others is inevitable. Take the case of Gauguin. He was a conventional Parisian banker and one day he packed it in and went to live in the South Sea islands, leaving his wife behind. Now who could say that a man who had such a tremendous artistic task to fulfil didn't act morally even though he undoubtedly hurt others in the process? I'm not, however, saying that one can do anything – that's the permissive society which I abhor. No, the question becomes whether one does only what is essential to one's own inner growth in a thoughtful and restrained manner to secure what one needs, or runs riot. My tycoon, for example, could have given up going on world tours with his mistress every year, out of consideration for his wife. There are cases where such behaviour can, at least it if it is conducted thoughtfully, in fact encourage the wife's independence and growth. But the real point is that every such situation is very precarious and individual and that it requires a creative decision, something which cannot be prescribed beforehand; it requires a tact and a wisdom of an intuitive order.'

'I must agree that the matter is delicate, otherwise I shouldn't have posed the problem. While I feel the rightness of what you are saying about the veritable law of inner growth with all the fibres of my personal being, I still question the imperiousness of this law. Here I should like to return to the matter of this man's *guilt* since I believe that something more than personal and socially-induced guilt-feelings are involved. Let me put it in the form of what will no doubt at first sight seem to be a very abstract question: Granted the law of personal fulfilment, can one find one's fulfilment alone, without involving others? Isn't there a certain individualism built into your formulation? Put the other way round, doesn't happiness inevitably include others and, if it does, then can there be fulfilment without regarding others?

I've formulated the problem in its most general form, because I want to go to the root of your friend's guilt. So I'd like, if I may, to pursue it a little at the same level. We can begin in a relatively simple way by turning to an article I came across in my capacity as English-language editor of an international theological journal. The article I have in mind was about Chinese ethics compared with Christian ethics. The author, Julia Ching, was talking about the central importance of the doctrine of *ren* (Jen), "human-heartedness", the moral virtue that makes a person truly human. She then went on:

> This word *ren*, itself a homophone of the word "human", is written with the radical "human" and another word signifying the number "two". It points to man's social nature, his relatedness to other men.[2]

These brief indications of Chinese thinking lit up for me what it is to be a human being: *being human intrinsically involves a reference to a second. Human-heartedness is an awareness of being half of two.* Couched in terms of the Chinese tradition, these two sentences nevertheless expressed an insight into human nature as such, universal human nature. We should therefore almost expect to find this perception recurring time and again in divers settings. I personally think immediately of two such expressions. The first is from the pen of the nineteenth

2. *Concilium* 150 (1981), at p.32.

century English idealist philosopher T.H. Green. He wrote as follows:

> The idea of the end or unconditioned good is that of the self as realised. And this self is *social*; the good includes that of others, who are also conceived as ends in themselves ... It [this social interest] implies the consciousness of a permanent well-being in which the permanent well-being of others is included.[3]

Essentially the same idea is developed in a peculary suggestive as well as personal way by the contemporary English legal philosopher John Finnis, who has done so much to recover and re-express the insight into natural law of Aristotle and Thomas Aquinas and who has, in the course of doing this, found a central place for the notion of *friendship*. He thinks of friendship as the working towards the maintenance of a new vantage point between the two friends:

> In friendship one is not thinking and choosing "from one's own point of view", nor from one's friend's point of view. Rather one is acting from a third point of view, the unique perspective from which one's own good and one's friend's good are equally "in view" and "in play".[4]

Do you see how all this helps us to understand your friend's guilt? These apparently high-flown abstractions allow us to see that what he was going against was not merely his socially-induced feelings but, in so far as he was not valuing his wife equally with himself, appraising things from the third point of view between them, he was going against his very nature. There is what might be called an ontology of guilt. In this connection, I should like to return to Schnitzler. For was it not his achievement as an artist to have been able to convey in

3. *Prologomenon to Ethics*, 4th ed. (1899), at p.xxvi.
4. *Natural Law and Natural Rights* (1980), at p.143.

convincing dramatic form the need of men and woman to be faithful for their very fulfilment, in the face of the urge to explore the darker side of their nature – even though it was also his tragedy as a human being that he was not able to live up to his insight but dissipated himself self-destructively in a multiplicity of relationships?'

'I absolutely agree with you when you talk about an ontology of guilt, Marcus, a going against the very order and structure of nature itself. At the same time I do want to insist that we have to go beyond text-books of moral theology and philosophy if we are to deal with the infinite complexity of real life, which is what makes an act of creative discernment imperative, an act which simply cannot be programmed in advance. Let me cite another sort of case. Since the case I want to mention concerns a mature woman, I should perhaps add that one of the complicating factors is that the creative decision I speak of is different at different ages while still being unpredictable. The problem of growth and morality is not the same in old age as it is in middle life or in youth. For in old age we need to retract our physical activities and go inwards, and the moral problem is what we owe our inner life and life itself. At the same time age does not dictate answers. Thus I have in my practice in the course of years met quite a number of woman who, at a comparatively advanced age, were still virgins. Many of them I had reason to admire for the great moral courage they showed in determining, often after a long agonising struggle, that it would be right to enter into a relationship with a man. The risk of an upheaval in the woman's personal life and subsequent unhappiness is always great. But the most trying decisions had to be made in cases where a deep and sincere love existed between the woman and a married man. I remember with particular admiration several women who, disregarding convention, ultimately entered into such relationships which I for my own part felt to be based on a truly moral decision.

What I'm saying, then, is that there are cases in which individuals have to go against the traditional morality in the interests of their own growth, and in which at best they live with the conflict until they have a sense of moral intuition from deep within, from the wisdom of the higher self. There the task of the counsellor is to help people to that maturing of the inner life from which the creative moral judgement can proceed.

My main point here, therefore, is that there are no ready-made answers, that such an act is creative and intuitive, a work of the subtlest moral tact and wisdom, countering anything that is merely subjective, self-seeking, tempestuous, and as such it is open to all human beings. It is a human answer to a human problem. I have, however, long thought that *this general human phenomenon is highlighted by the case of so many artists* – and here I'm talking about great artists. The essential moral conflict may be the same but it occurs in an intense form in them. Let me give you a few examples.

Wagner is widely acknowledged to be a composer of genius. Yet in his private life he was a liar, a cheat, an egomaniac and an adulterer. He lied to King Ludwig and he stole Cosima Bülow from his best friend. He was utterly dependent on this woman in his life, confessing himself unable to work when she was away. Thus as a human being he was pathetic, even repulsive, and yet he did all these despicable things for the sake of achieving his works of art, which must surely be accounted masterpieces.

The case of Toscanini is perhaps even more interesting. He was a very intense and emotional man, a veritable force of nature, a conductor of radiant energy and genius. His performances were so demanding and high-powered that he had to have release. It is a fact that he had numerous and often tempestuous love-affairs, some casual, some not so casual. In his case he could not fail to be aware that he was transgressing traditional morality. There was one famous occasion when the leading soprano, an Italian woman, who was pregnant by him, was howled at on the stage. Another of his mistresses asked him to leave his wife, he flatly refused and the affair broke up. He allowed himself this freedom. With all this power and intensity he could not have remained a faithful husband in a conventional sense, he was an artist. Yet he remained utterly committed to the idea of indissolubility of marriage. So he remained with his wife, Carla, to the end. Not only that, it is one of the most intriguing features of his character that he rejected divorce so much that, if any of his friends did divorce, he never spoke to them again!'

'What did his wife feel about all this, Martin?'

'I think that basically she accepted the situation. She was a very calm, loyal, motherly woman, certainly not an exciting woman. Many women in such circumstances either are relieved because as a result the demands on them are less or else they just accept things. At the same time, I must admit that there always will be tension, there will always be pain on both sides, and guilt on at least one, not least some guilt on the wife's part for not being adequate. On the other hand, what would have been the alternative in, say, Toscanini's case? Suppression of his needs would have been disastrous to his artistic activities, let alone to him as a human being. Who is the better for it? A wife in such cases also has to be realistic and has to accept the best possible compromise in all the circumstances. They must seek a compromise which is least hurtful to both.

But let me go back to my next case, that of Georges Simenon. I must admit that I'm an addict, and I hope it isn't for that reason that I regard him as a great writer. He is, of course, famous for his invention of the character of Maigret but he has written numerous other novels, touched into convincing life not only by his native penetration but by that voracious reading of books of psychology which is almost an obsession with him. They have a spontaneity and an inevitability which few other writers achieve. Do you know how he works? He is an extremely sensual man and cannot begin until he has been stimulated by some immediate sensation: a sound, a smell, a touch, an impression of light. This need, this artistic need amounting almost to an obsession with sensuality, has conditioned his whole way of life and his creative process. It is said about him that when a novel starts to stir in him, he seems to fall ill, and to become feverish, as with 'flu. The doctor may be called in and he says: "It's not 'flu, its a novel." Simenon then withdraws and writes for, say, eight to ten days and nights, almost non-stop. But once he has finished, then, in order to relieve the tension but also in order to reconnect with the lower, the crudely sensual element which he had taken up into the creative process, in the words of a fellow artist he just rushes to the brothel. He is said to have had thousands of women, as well as having gone through three wives. It could of course be said that he overdid it, for, as somebody else said, he has the sexual habits of a commercial traveller. But the point is that sensual stimulation, even at the expense of conventional morality, was indispensable for his artistic being. In this respect, then, he was like Mozart, for he is the very by-word for the sublime and yet he could be very crude, even obscene in his behaviour and language because he needed to keep in touch with life even in its grossest form in order to remain creative. So again you see the predicament in moral terms, since he surely had an obligation to his art, and the problem of growth here is that of a person's growth as an artist.'

'I do take your point, Martin, that the case of the artist is a more vivid version of the conflict which many people experience between demands from within and demands from without, and I do agree that it is perhaps even more of a genuinely moral conflict than the case of other people in so far as a great work of art as an enhancement of life has a moral value in itself. I must admit that I do also have certain reservations. There is first of all the fact that your way of thinking and presentation are somewhat Romantic. Wasn't it your beloved Goethe himself who wrote out of his experience of the essentially Romantic *Sturm und Drang* and his refinding of the classical mood:

Wer Grosses will muss sich zusammen raffen.
In der Beschränkung zeigt sich erst der Meister

Und das Gesetz nur kann uns Freiheit geben.[5]

This is rendered by Michael Hamburger as follows:

Who seeks great gain leaves easy gain behind.
None proves a master but by limitation,
And only law can give us liberty.

While he himself may not have been able to live up to the ideal glimpsed here, are there not more Classical artists who were, such as Milton, Bach, Jane Austin, Gerard Manly Hopkins?

There is something deeper which lies behind this reservation on my part. It's simply that I wonder whether you do not allow a place for an ideal of complete fidelity to commitments, whatever the cost? Isn't living for an ideal also a basic need?'

'I not only allow for such a need, Marcus, I give it *a quite central place*. Striving for the ideal is the supreme need, and for me anything else is only an approach to it. The supreme need of man is to be faithful to his higher self, which inevitably demands restraint and sacrifice. Even Schnitzler was able to practice these virtues in his artistic life, though not in his personal life. But even this conflict points to the fact that what we're talking about is a *process* – of *slow redemption*. People may have to live through the darkness and terror of some more or less orgiastic outburst before they can be liberated. So for me what I've previously called "schöpferische Verzicht", creative renunciation, is the proto-phenomenon of human experience – that a man can be confronted with temptation but reject it. A simple example is the case of Galsworthy. As you may well know, he fell in love with a woman of eighteen when he was at the dangerous age of forty, but he said "No" because he wanted to remain faithful to his wife. What one has to do as a counsellor in any such situation is to assess whether there is any possibility of such a renunciation, any substance of strength to attempt this, and, if there is the slightest chance of

5. from a poem beginning 'Natur und
   Kunst ...'

mobilising it, to challenge the person and to make the approach to the higher self. But in many cases this strength is not there, while the unlived life is very much there to torment a man or woman. In this case one just has to make the best possible, the least hurtful, the least self-seeking, the least subjective compromise. But may I repeat: the central case of human experience is the pursuit of the ideal. Any deviation is only a stepping-stone to the ultimate ideal.'

'Well, Martin, if you say this, then you've completely answered my initial question in so far as I talked about a tension and you have now spoken, and so vitally, about both terms of this tension. You began by arguing the need to follow what you called the law of one's inner being, you then stressed the central importance of the pursuit of the ideal, and so you have stated a reconciliation of principle, albeit in terms of process, struggle and pain.'

'Yes, and in this connection, Marcus, there is a brief saying of Christian Morgenstern, that poetic philosopher or philosophical poet, which perfectly sums up for me what you have expressed in those last words: process, struggle and pain. He once wrote a poem to guilt and addressed it as "Schuld, du dunkle Huld", "guilt, thou dark blessing".[6] You see, what he saw was that even guilt – guilt in what you call the ontological sense of hurting one's deepest self and life itself – guilt as suffering from doing even what one has to do, can be a stepping-stone to redemption, to a greater freedom, to the attainment of the ideal.'

'You know, Martin, I find this statement of your position wholly acceptable, and you may be surprised to learn that it happens to be, to my mind, a spontaneous recovery and personalised restatement of the teaching of Thomas Aquinas. For he says, in two crucial successive articles of his *Summa Theologiae* on conscience, that while one is bound to follow one's conscience, even it it is mistaken, one is not thereby necessarily excused from fault. You see, in his dry scholastic

6. 'An die Schuld', in *Epigramme und Sprüche*.

7. la. q. 19, articles 5 and 6.

way he too holds a balance between inner conviction and what I call ontological reality, nature, the objective order of things, what you tend to call certain basic, unalterable laws.'

'I didn't of course know that, Marcus, but naturally I'm delighted to be on the side of the angelic doctor!'

'Not only this time, Martin. May I take this further, and again, I'm sorry to say, in a more philosophic direction.

You know only too well that there is a great deal of talk nowadays about a new morality. It is couched at a more popular level in terms of the permissive society, at a more esoteric level in terms of the Aquarian age. I take it, however, from what you say that you, like me, are in favour of a new morality in the sense of investing the traditional codes with a deeper and a more personal meaning, regarding them as expressions of what you have here referred to as the law of inner growth, but that you are not in favour of it in the sense of sanctioning the pursuit of more or less untutored intuitions and wishes. I ask you for your opinion on this topic because I think that this division represents one of the great conflicts of value-judgement in our time.

As I see it, one value system believes centrally in *experience*. More and more widely people, and especially young people, are saying that they rely on experience to guide them through life rather than any code or tradition or the advice of others. This expresses at once a disillusionment with received systems and some sort of faith in their own creativity. "Experience" is thus one of the great words of our time, almost a rallying cry, a shibboleth of modernity. I recently had two pungent experiences of this – if I may use the word! Somebody was saying to me just the other day that she liked our previous book because it was based on experience, and two days later I happened to be distributing communion to a student when I noticed that the word machine-stitched above the pocket of her denim jacket was : "Experience" ... But I think of two more generalised expressions of this trend of thinking and feeling. One of the clearest I know of is Erich Fromm's in his justly acclaimed little book *The Art of Loving*, first published in Great Britain in 1957 but reprinted many times since:

> While irrational faith is rooted in submission to a power which is felt to be overwhelmingly strong, omniscient and omnipotent, and in the abdication of one's own power and strength, rational faith is based upon the opposite experience. We have this faith in a thought because it is the result of our own observation and thinking. We have faith in the potentialities of others, of ourselves, and of mankind because, and only to the degree to which, we have experienced the growth of our own potentialities, the reality of growth in ourselves, the strength of our own power of reason and of love.[8]

Carl Rogers speaks in a very similar vein in his *On Becoming a Person*:

> *Experience is, for me, the highest authority.* The touchstone of validity is my own experience. No other person's idea, and none of my own ideas, are as authoritative as my experience. It is to experience that I must return again and again, to discover a closer approximation to truth as it is in the process of becoming in me.
>
> Neither the Bible nor the prophets – neither Freud nor research – neither the revelations of God nor man – can take precedence over my own inner experience.[9]

Now experience is a notion that is not only very familiar but one that is very rich and intricate. It's only in our time that people are beginning to analyse the notion more systematically and they're finding it very complex. It's like what St Augustine said about time: We know what it is until someone asks us to define it ... I cannot therefore hope to do justice to it. There do, however appear to be at least two essential

8. at pp.103-104.
9. at pp.23-24. The italics are the author's own.

elements in the ordinary notion of experience: it somehow means both what one has learned *already*, some deposit from this past ("in my experience") and also something new that one encounters, something one has *yet* to learn ("its all experience"). There is a phrase in one of the leading studies of this and associated notions that hits off the presence of these two elements and the mysterious tension between them: "that strange fusion of memory and expectation into a whole that we name experience and that we acquire from experience"[10].

Thus when we appeal to experience we may have in mind something we have indeed experienced and so we do so with the thought of the element of the remembered past, or we may have in mind something yet to be encountered, and so we do so with the thought of the other element in the notion of experience, that of the new, or else we may have in mind something new to complement the past and so we do so with the thought of the new somehow of a piece with the past. It is precisely the apparent permission in the notion of experience to slip imperceptibly from one element to the other that constitutes a great deal of its plausibility. But reliance on the past imprisons one in that past and so is a limited guide, reliance on what is new is by definition reliance on something unknown and so cannot count as a guide, *at least in the same sense*, while reliance on what is new on the basis of what has gone before begs the question of how the new relates to the past. The very amalgam of past and new, memory and expectation thus hides the fact that the two main elements are disparate so that slipping from one element to the other to escape from the limitations of either is a logically illegitimate jump and the plausibility is spurious. This is why for me reliance on experience above all, in the spirit of Erich Fromm and Carl Rogers, is at the very least logically incoherent.

It is no doubt because of even the logical inadequacy of the notion of experience to take the full weight of being a guide and "authority" and "touchstone" of life that Cardinal Newman made an apologia for accepting the inevitability and

10. *Truth and Method* (1975), at p.195.

the desirability of relying on guidance from the past, therefore from some tradition and some inherited code of belief and behaviour, though without thereby disallowing a place for experience. In, for instance, *An Essay on the Development of Christian Doctrine* and the *University Sermons* he referred to the presumptive character of so much of our actual life – the fact that we live out of the past, some pre-shaping of the new, out of anticipations, acceptance and hence out of *trust*: "we must begin by believing and ... conviction will follow".[11] The essence of the alternative value system, therefore, is the frank and willing acceptance of some pre-guidance, some tutoring and directing of our projects, prejudice in the etymological sense of pre-judice, pre-judgement, *Vorverständnis* or pre-understanding. On this view we acknowledge the complex of received and learned attitudes and information with which we inevitably come to anything fresh, albeit only as an initiation which then *does* need to be tested in experience and so personally appropriated into conviction. Since such living initially out of trust is not irrational, then neither is the supreme case of such trust, namely, trust in what we take to be revelation by God himself. We then believe in order to understand, trust in order to become convinced, presume in order to experience.

So far I have tried to state the conflict of value systems in my own words and in terms of spokesmen of the Anglo-American tradition. In fact the conflict is a very profound one, as has been shown massively by the man whom I quoted a few minutes ago, the disciple of Heidegger, the German philosopher Hans-Georg Gadamer. In *Truth and Method* he describes the conflict I am indicating in terms of the running and continuing battle between the values of, on the one hand, reason, experience and individualism, and on the other, tradition, pre-understanding, pre-judice, faith in revelation that set in for us with the Enlightenment of the eighteenth century.

11. Pelican Classics, 1974, p.343.

Not that this is an exclusively modern or even a Western problem. I was fascinated to discover recently that no less a person that Mahatma Ghandi experienced the conflict between faith and conscience, what we are here calling social morality and inner growth, acutely in his own life and person, though he experienced it against the background of the antique acceptance of a traditional code, in his case the eternal law expressed in the Vedas of India. This is how R.C. Zaehner puts it in his book *Hinduism*:

> In his frail person the ancient ideal of renunciation, "harmlessness" (*ahimsa*, translated by him as "non-violence") and truth met. He described himself as a *sanatani* Hindu, one who follows the *sanatana dharma*, the "eternal law" once embodied in the *dharma-raja*, Yudishthira. Ghandi's dilemma was the same as Yudishthira's: what and where *was* the *sanatana dharma* he claimed to follow? Was it in the heart or was it in what the Brahmans proclaimed? ...
>
> So it seemed only natural that he could say of the scriptures, "My belief in the Hindu Scriptures does not require me to accept every word and every verse as divinely inspired. Nor do I claim to have any first-hand knowledge of these wonderful books. But I do claim to know and feel the truths of the essential teaching of the Scriptures. I decline to be bound by any interpretation, however learned it may be, if it is repugnant to reason and moral sense." The outraged conscience of Yudishthira speaks through the lips of Mahatma Ghandi.[12]

This way of putting it reminds us in the Judaeo-Christian tradition of those extraordinarily revolutionary but yet traditional words of Jesus: "You leave the commandment of God, and hold fast the tradition of men."[13] It is as if he were saying that God's own teaching can come to us only through the

12. at pp.170-171.
13. Mark 7:7.

vehicle of man's teaching and yet this very mediation can distort and betray it. The archetypal teaching therefore needs to be disengaged and rediscovered time and time again, in a searching interplay between trust and experience, code and conscience – but, I should say, and I think that here you agree with me, on the basis of an *initial* and initiating acceptance of the tradition and the moral code.'

'Yes, Marcus, I do indeed agree with you. For me there *are* certain basic and unalterable laws. These belong to the perfected moral nature of man, his higher self. For instance, adultery remains adultery and the higher self does not commit adultery. I do not want to sanctify and make permanent any deviation from these basic laws. What a counsellor does is to help a client to move, by slow stages, towards this ideal, and he has to accept compromise solutions, tentative answers which have to do with the lower self, developmental obstacles, and so on, but which can stimulate and promote growth. But these are only stepping-stones towards the ideal.'

'So you give a very interesting twist to the notion of movement towards an ideal in so far as you say that a counsellor has not merely to tolerate but in some sense to encourage what you call compromise solutions which fall short of the ideal, *provided* that they can be seen to stimulate efforts to grow beyond them ...'

'And ultimately leave them behind. Then the tension is ultimately resolved.'

'I see, Martin. You know that what you now say reminds me of a distinction which has long been made in the Roman Catholic tradition and which was one of the first things which Cardinal Hume recalled after becoming archbishop of Westminster. This is the distinction between principle and pastoral application. He said that we have to be uncompromising on principle and infinitely flexible on application. This is the real pastoral skill, so that what you are talking about is as it were the secular equivalent of this pastoral skill.'

'What you say is most interesting, Marcus, and not only for its immediate content. For in comparing the counsellor to the priest you remind me of the contrast between their two roles which you drew at the beginning of this morning's discussion and so also of something I've thought for a long time. You see, for me the counsellor and the priest have different tasks and different resources. The priest has the possibility of addressing and challenging this higher self which is inactive or only partially awake and of doing so directly, and he has the resources of the sacred text, the sacraments, prayers, his whole presence, even his appearance and dress as a pointer to something beyond his individual and limited self. The counsellor, on the other hand, starts from the other end; his business is to help sort out the problems of the lower self in the way we've seen this morning, and he doesn't have the office or role – or the image – of challenging the higher self directly which the priest has; he can only open the way to the other becoming more receptive to the presence and influence of the higher self. Priest and counsellor, therefore, work together, but from different directions – and, of course, the priest-counsellor has in principle both resources, like yourself.'

'I appreciate your saying that, Martin, but I have in all conscience to say that in actual practice when I'm using counselling skills in the course of performing my priestly role, I find that discernment of what emphasis I am to give in any concrete case very delicate to make. I find it difficult to know from which end I'm to begin, at what time I'm to make the challenge of which you speak so justly. I must also say that in my experience one can make a mistake in either direction: either confronting the other with the spiritual challenge too soon or allowing him to continue in his experiments too long. Here too one has to accept the possibility of making mistakes. Perhaps the essential thing is to allow any sense of the infinite complexity of human situations and of the human struggle to be charged with the spirit of that statement of St Paul which you have quoted to me before: "Not that I am already perfect: but I press on ... forgetting what lies behind and straining forward to what lies ahead."[14] The key-word here is "straining

14. Philippians 3:12-13.

forward", and I find it most interesting that it is precisely this passage and *this word* in particular which St Gregory of Nyssa, in his *Life of Moses*, uses to develop his novel idea of perfection as a continual progress. If we wanted to invent a word, we could shape it from the Greek original of "straining forward", *epekteinomai*, and say that we have to retain a sense of man's life being "epekteinic", a matter of ceaselessly straining forward.'

'I quite agree. In my own terms the conflicts, the crises, the moments of decision, the darkness and the terror, the very guilt cannot be what I've called stepping-stones towards the ideal of the higher self unless a person has been alerted to it, is future-oriented, otherwise he'll just settle down and feel comfortable. But for me the other side of this coin is that one can also overstrain oneself. I remember a woman of my aquaintance saying so often "Why can't I be perfect, why can't I be perfect?" For myself I accept what human nature is, I accept what I am. I just ask myself what the next step is, and I accept the struggle.'

'I'm reminded of a succinct statement of Carl Rogers, and since I quoted him before in order to disagree with him, I'd like to cite him now, since this time I endorse what he says:

> I believe that I have learned this from my clients as well as within my own experience – that we cannot change, we cannot move away from what we are, until we thoroughly *accept* what we are. Then change seems to come about almost unnoticed.[15]

This in turn recalls another passage which is very similar in meaning but which is couched in more dramatic and more religious terms. It is from Harry Williams' fine little book *The True Wilderness*:

> Human life is very largely a wilderness, a dry land where

15. at p.17. The italics are the author's own.

no water is ... once we thus accept our wilderness and no longer try to hide it from ourselves, there follows the miracle of resurrection. The desert become verdant. The stony ground itself brings forth rich pastures. It is, for instance, the man who faces and accepts his inability to love who discovers within himself a power of loving which nothing external can destroy or diminish. This is life through death.'[16]

'I for my part, Marcus, can wholly accept both these statements. Thank you very much.'

16. at p.12.

Dialogue 5:
Sex and
Contemplation

Love is an elemental means of self-satisfaction and a
physical avenue, apart from mystical immersion, to
possible transcendence.

Rainer Maria Rilke Siegfried Mandel[1]

As in the *Śaiva Siddhānta* so in the Gītā and Rāmānaja
God imprisons souls in matter only to release them and
unite them with himself. This constitutes his adorable
'game' (*krida, lila*).

Hinduism R.C.Zaehner[2]

'The subject I should like to discuss with you today, Martin, is
one which we have touched upon from time to time explicitly,
and this is no doubt because in its essence it pervades
everything we talk about. For our underlying theme, just as
human beings, even more than in the roles we play out to and
for each other as counsellor and priest, is *relationship and
spirituality* under different aspects, and sex and contemplation
are the intensest forms of these two things. They also sum up
the paradox of relationship and spirituality because while sex
and contemplation seem to be at emnity with each other, there
is a recurrent intuition throughout history that they are also
very close to each other. What is the truth of the matter?

When I ask for the truth of the matter, I mean, of course,
practical not speculative or academic truth, because nothing

1. at p.121.
2. at p.99.

96

could be more personal to each of us than our sexuality and our possible openness to what St Augustine unforgettably called the God who is "more intimate to us than we are to ourselves". It is at this level that I should like to put the question to you this morning.

For the subject is in the first place quite obviously of personal interest not only to me as a man but because I am a celibate member of a contemplative Order and so experience the problem in terms of a struggle within my own body and person. Yet I continue to try to pray, and I feel the need to experience life contemplatively, to make sense of it, even of frustration, pain, tragedy and sin as a very important need too. I value the opportunity to talk the problem over with you, especially as I assume that you experience similar tensions within yourself but from the different point of view of a man who has a happily married life of almost fifty years behind him and yet is also passionately committed to meditation and contemplation.

Moving to a more general level, I again see the subject of sex and contemplation in terms of a series of dilemmas or tensions. Thus, in the first place, we need Freud only to remind us, not to tell us, what so much experience and so much of the world's art testifies, namely, that sexual attraction is one of the great forces which moves the world, and that we fail to acknowledge it at our peril. On the other hand, we also know intuitively – which was surely part of the message of Freud himself – that an unregulated pursuit of sex is incompatible with being human, let alone with gaining access to the contemplative possibilities of our nature. Then again, to take the question from another angle, we may acknowledge that man is capable of contemplation, in fact that he deeply needs to contemplate in order to come to the unfailing source of his being and find the true love of his heart, and yet the experience of both of us in dealing with people who aspire to spirituality is that one of the most insidious traps on their path, is a denial of their sexuality and bodiliness and so a premature spirituality and a false sublimation. So where is discernment and sanity in this matter? But perhaps this is enough to introduce the topic I have in mind?'

'It certainly is, Marcus, and I'd better stop you here so that I can begin to respond. And since you began yourself in so personal a vein, I'd like to begin myself by acknowledging a comparable tension in my own life. Now you put your own position as a celibate priest in the foreground of your introductory remarks, and this is of course only one aspect of the whole subject you have raised this morning. But since you have mentioned it, you may be surprised to learn that my contemplative nature asserted itself early in my life in so far as I wished to be celibate from my very teens. You know, in my school days I used to get up several times in the night pretending to be a monk with my bible! In retrospect I now think that this may, at least in part, have been a reaction to what I saw of sex in earliest childhood. Such an experience of sex as ugly and distasteful is, of course, far from unique. Many people have such shadows over their sexuality.

One case which occurs to me is that of Mahler. As a young man he was living as a lodger in poor digs in Vienna and one day he came upon a fellow lodger, Alfred Grünfeld, a pianist, later to become famous, in the act of intercourse with the serving girl. Mahler was so appalled by what he found repulsive and *tierisch*, bestial, that he tried to haul the fellow off from the girl. He got a very bad reception and was sent packing. Whether this was the only cause, or only a factor, he certainly had a block about sex which later made itself felt in his relationship with Alma, his wife, twenty years younger than himself and one of the greatest beauties in Vienna when he married her. It was a difficult marriage and it is interesting that Mahler consulted Freud. Now Freud, you know, was a man of very regular habits who also insisted on taking his holidays which he much enjoyed. So when Mahler got in touch, Freud agreed to see him only on condition that Mahler accompanied him on one of his holiday walks. Mahler agreed and went, they walked for four hours, and Mahler felt much better about his relationship to Alma – whether as a result of what Freud said, or of what he just was, no one will ever know.

Anyhow, the point is that many of us have such dark experiences of sexuality. I certainly did, but apart from possibly inducing in me this almost life-long desire to be celibate, my childhood experience also aroused my sexual awareness very early. I long hoped that I would "overcome" sex, but one of the lessons of my life is that few, if any, can; certainly that I could not, and I just had to accept this. Sex is, of course, complex, and is readily confused with desire, which can make us feel guilty, but sex is not the same as desire. It can manifest itself as desire, but it first manifests itself at the lowest level simply as hunger, a need as physiological as hunger in the ordinary sense, which is how the Buddha spoke of it.

My question, therefore, becomes that of knowing how to manage this dual need – to reconcile a life-long need for contemplation with the need for sexual release, and here my personal question becomes a typical one. How to do justice to human nature and not stifle it, in such a way as to keep it in balance with a socially ordered and moral life that hurts neither others nor oneself and so retain one's mental and spiritual integrity and independence. Above all, how is one to arrange one's life so as not to suffer intolerable intrusions into one's contemplative life?

I've thought a great deal about this and lived it through in my own life, compared my own experience with other's and I've come to certain conclusions. In the first place, I believe that in order to be fully human everybody must awaken to sexuality and go through a basic sexual experience in youth, in the way that, for instance, the Buddha and St Augustine did. This learning experience or basic experience by itself liberates human potential. So far as the next phase in life is concerned, in my opinion, as I've already indicated, one must have a sexual partner, but if one also seriously wants to lead a contemplative life one's choice of such a partner is crucial. In this regard I have in my professional life dealt with more marital problems than with any other sort of problem and so I've come across couples who have experienced all the famed delights and ecstasies of sex but who, to my complete astonishment, have in most cases experienced little or no human contact or communication in their love-making and, even more, are usually not given to contemplation. It's as if we could not experience everything in human nature. Certainly, for me personally, frequent and passionate excitement and the experience of delirious ecstasy is incompatible with any serious and sustained contemplative life, whereas the relief of basic sexual need, human contact, mutual helpfulness, companionship and the sharing of interests is conducive to it.'

'So it's as if there were several possible combinations of sexual and contemplative activities which could be thought of as forming a continuum – sexual ecstasy, settled domesticity, marital contemplation, celibate contemplation, Martin?'

'Exactly, Marcus, we have to establish our priorities and if we want to lead a contemplative, as well as sexual life, we have to choose a partner accordingly.

That, however, in not all that is necessary. A sexual comradeship must also be lived in the context of what I've previously called a *serene way of life* generally – refraining from unnecessary talking and blethering; ensuring quiet spaces during the day, especially before seeing anyone professionally; taking a minimum of bodily exercise; chastening one's senses; as far as possible keeping free from the overstimulation and titillation of the media; a suitable diet. This amounts to an ascetic, but not, I think, an unnatural way of life. This is the sort of way in which I envisage the appeasement of the passions in the interests of a contemplative life – the modest equivalent of the way in which St Jerome was able to study in his cell because the lion of his feelings had settled down quietly at his feet, next to his dog, as depicted in the engraving by Albrecht Dürer which I keep just inside the door of the room we are in, as you may have noticed.'

'As a matter of fact, I've often observed your other pictures as well as all the books here but I've never noticed this engraving, Martin, and I must make good my oversight when I leave this morning. But your discreet reference to the classical precedent only increases the fascination I felt on hearing you describe what you call the serene way of life that, in your opinion, is a necessary foundation and setting for a contemplative life. For what was passing through my mind as you spoke was another classical reference – St Thomas Aquinas' analysis of the inter-relationship between the active and the contemplative life in general and between the act of contemplation strictly so called, *simplex intuitus veritatis*, the "simple intuition of the truth", and the manner of ordering one's emotions and way of life and the very life of the imagination which dispose a man to this contemplation in particular. But all this teaching was put more accessibly and engagingly by Fr Victor White OP in the admirable little commentary which he composed for one quantitatively tiny but qualitatively rich work of St Thomas, namely, the letter of advice on how to study which he wrote to a young Dominican student, Brother John. This is how Fr Victor White rendered his master's teaching:

> The natural desire to know of Brother John's mind must not be weakened, still less deadened; it is this that will provide the needed motivation for all his studies. But moderated – not in our sense of diluted, but in St Thomas's sense of being given "modus", order, direction – it must be. If Brother John wants to attain wisdom, he must not be impatient, in a hurry. It is slow work, and it cannot be done by cramming or by any slick technique. This may be damping and disappointing; but if Brother John thinks so, then there is worse to follow.
> For two thirds of the remainder of the letter seem to have nothing to do with intellectual, scientific method at all. Brother John had asked how to *study*; St Thomas replies by telling him how to *live*. He continues: "Haec est ergo

3. He does this in questions 180 and 183 of the 2a., 2ae., of his great *Summa Theologica*.

monitio mea de *vita tua*" ["This, therefore, is my advice on how you are to live"]. That "ergo" therefore, must seem strangely inconsequential until we remember what St Thomas, developing some ideas in Aritotle's Ethics, has to say about the relation of the life of virtue to the life of contemplation. *Essentialiter* [essentially] moral virtue had nothing to so with science, with the search for truth; but *dispositive, removens prohibens* [dispositively, by way of the removal of obstacles] it is indispensable: "For the act of contemplation is impeded both by the vehemence of the emotions, by which the attention of the soul is drawn from the things of the mind to the things of sense, and also by external disturbances. But it is precisely the task of the moral virtues to prevent the immoderate vehemence of the emotions, and to quieten the disturbances arising from the external business."[4]

So instead of some elaborate methodologico-pedagogical technique, what Brother John gets first of all from the great Master Thomas is a list of matter-of-fact commonplaces which he might have got any day from his novice-master. He must be careful about keeping silence, he must be slow to speak; he must embrace purity of conscience; he must not cease to spend plenty of time in prayer. Also, he must keep to his cell, love his cell ... He must think twice before wandering off to the common room; he must be on amicable terms with his companions, neither aloof from any nor too familiar with any; and he must not get himself entangled in the affairs of outsiders. Above all he must avoid "discursus" – which perhaps we can best translate by "rushing about" in the colloquial sense – and imitate the examples of the saints and other sound men ...

I confess that when I first read this letter, I was surprised that St Thomas, in this context of study, laid such emphasis on *fraternal charity*, and Brother John's attitude

4. 2a., 2ae., question 180, article 2.

to his companions. But one cannot have lived for twenty years in houses of study without realising to how great an extent study is helped by satisfactory or hindered by mismanaged personal relationships ... A vigorous sense-life is not merely, for the student, a condescending concession to his "lower nature", it is a necessity for his studies themselves ...[5]

You see? Leaving aside the question of celibacy, which is a special problem, as you've indicated already yourself, it's as if you had out of your own experience of yourself and others spontaneously formulated a secular version of a monastic way of life ... !

There is, however, one problem about your account of the way of life that is the necessary setting for contemplative activities. As you spoke, I was thinking of various people I have come across who were so restless and active that they just could not tolerate the regime of life which you and St Thomas describe. Nor is this only my own personal question. I'm again encouraged in this thought by recalling the perception of one of the witnesses St Thomas Aquinas quoted in this same sequence of reflections on the contemplative life, Pope St Gregory called the Great:

It often happens that those who have been quite decently occupied in leading an ordinary human life have been slain by the sword of quiet ... There are some people who are so restless that they begin to feel crushed when they stop working, because the more leisure they have the more exasperated they become by the tumult of their heart.

St Thomas accepts this and says that "those who are liable to feel things intensely because they are temperamentally active are sometimes better suited to the active than to the

5. at pp.18-19, 21, 23.

contemplative life", whereas those who "are constitutionally quiet and calm are better suited for contemplation", to the point that they deteriorate if they are required to do nothing but work.[6]

You see, I think that we need to have the discernment of a St Gregory and a St Thomas if we are not to run the risk of extending a way of life which happens to suit you and me to people whom it might not suit, in fact whom it would definitely aggravate.'

'I quite agree with you there, Marcus. I've already said that every person is unique, and that different people need different solutions. People do need to identify their own disposition. I would, however, in the first place like to say that everybody, even the most active person, has at least the potential for contemplation somewhere within him and so needs, if not space for contemplation in any strict sense, then at least what I call some "quiet time". Lotz has the wonderful image of the wheel which turns at its periphery but the axle of which remains still at the centre. Unless we find the still centre we shall only turn at the periphery. I do think that some minimum of withdrawal, standing back from the press of acitivity, some stillness, recollection, is necessary for leading any life that can be called human.

Subject to this, however, I accept what you – and your illustrious predecessors – say. In fact I'd take it further, because for me the fundamental reason why the balance of activity and quiet must be adjusted to each individual is that we are dealing not merely with sexual impulses but with *every sort of disordered impulse* – what the Buddhists call "cravings" and what St John of the Cross calls "appetites". There may be appetites for, most simply, food, for restless movement, for power, or even for intellectual gratification, as well as for sex. It is such appetites we need to subdue and silence, these are the beasts we need to tame. I remember two lines of Goethe:

Wass euch das innere stört

6. in question 183, article 4.

Sollt ihr nicht leiden

"What perturbs your inner being, you should not suffer to happen" – whatever it may be. It is, therefore, just because this is so that I agree that work can for many people, perhaps for most people, be a most important way of combating their cravings. For any intense work, and certainly work with people, uses up two things: first, one's physical vitality – one simply gets tired, exhausted even; and, secondly, in the case of caring work, one's energy and resources of loving and caring. I certainly find myself that I'm much less conditioned by sexual demands when I work as hard as possible. Further such a giving and receiving of love is itself a redemption of even the sexual impulse.'

'I'm glad you go below the surface of the subject, Martin, and that you now state that your "serene way of life" and work is in fact a matter of an implacable battle with the deepest and darkest desires and fears of man's nature. I'm also very glad that you make at least a sidelong reference to the tradition of the East by your use of the term "cravings". For it seems to me that we're now talking about something central to the spiritual traditions of both West and East.

At first sight it seems that the traditions of West and East are strikingly similar. Thus in the West a distinction is made between the active and the contemplative life and they are variously symbolised by the figures of Leah and Rachel, Martha and Mary, Peter and John. The Eastern tradition similarly distinguishes between the way of knowledge or wisdom (*jñāna*) and the way of action (*karma*). Thus, for example, the *Bhagavad Gītā* says:

> In this world there are two roads of perfection, as I told thee before, O prince without sin: Jñāna Yoga, the path of wisdom of the Sankhyas, and Karma Yoga, the path of action of the yogis.[7]

7. III, 3, in the translation of Juan Mascaró.

When we come to look at the matter more closely, however, and see how the masters of either tradition seek to state how these two ways relate to each other and work out in practice, we become aware of a subtle but very important difference, it seems to me. For, on the one hand, two of the great masters of the West do not just state the distinction but do so in the context of ranking them in relation to each other. Thus St Augustine writes in *The City of God*:

> The love of truth seeks holy leisure (*otium sanctum*), but the compelling force of love accepts due busyness. If nobody imposes this latter burden on you, give yourself up to the pursuit and intuition of truth. If it is imposed, however, you should take it up out of the compulsion of love. And yet you should not completely desert the delight of truth, lest you lose its sweetness and become crushed by activity.[8]

St Thomas sums up his teaching in the very article in which he quotes this passage:

> We have to say that, simply speaking, the contemplative life is better than the active.[9]

On the other hand, Eastern texts state the distinction but leave the relationship between the respective terms unstated. Thus the *Bhagavad Gītā* says, for instance, the following:

> Stand fast in Yoga, surrending attachment;
> In success and failure be the same,
> And then get busy with thy works.

8. Book XIX, quoted in the *Summa*, in
   question 182, article 1, in the reply
   to the third question.
9. 2a., 2ae., question 182, article 1.

Yoga means "sameness" and "indifference" (*samatva*).[10]

Better one's own duty (*dharma*) [to perform], though
void of merit,
Than to do another's well:
Better to die within [the sphere of] one's own duty:
Perilous is the duty of other men.[11]

The teaching here implied is well summed up by Zaehner in
his *Hinduism*:

In the Bhagavad Gītā three paths to the Absolute are
offered to the man who seeks liberation – the path of
"knowledge" (*jñāna*), the path of action (*karma*), and the
path of *bhakti*. By "knowledge" is understood not simply
book-learning, which according to the Upanishads leads
you nowhere, but the intuitive apprehension of Brāhman
– a term which is variously interpreted by the philo-
sophers but which in the Gītā means the direct
apprehension of the timeless Reality and the inter-
connection of all things as cohering in the "great Self"
and therefore also in the individual "self" once it is
liberated from its mortal bonds. To speak of a "path of
action" as far as the Gītā is concerned is misleading, for
this does not mean that the active life, as against the
contemplative, has value of its own but that it is possible
and desirable to pursue the life of contemplation while
still engaged in an active life, be it the sacred ministration
of the Brāhman, the warfare of the Kshatriya, the
business activity of the Vaiśya, or the menial service of
the Śūdra. All these activities are good and each of the
four great classes should carry out the duties of their
station, for this is the *dharma* prescribed by the law books

10. Book II, 48.
11. Book III, 35, both in the translation of R.C. Zaehner.

and the will of God, but the zealous performance of caste can never lead to liberation, for action breeds its own reward or punishment, and the 'fruits' or *karma* bind whether they be good or bad; they 'attach' to good or evil and therefore militate against detachment which is the *sine qua non* of liberation ... [12]

Thus the West gives a priority to the contemplative life but does so in making it alternate with the active life in a way that the East does not, whereas the East at first seems to put the active and the contemplative life on a par only then to suggest that it is, in Zaehner's key words, possible and desirable to "pursue the life of contemplation while still engaged in an active life", which suggests an effective priority of the contemplative life over the active after all. The initial similarity seems on closer inspection to dissolve and this is all the more puzzling as a basic agreement seems nevertheless to lie hidden somehow in the very blurring.

The way to unravel this tangle would seem to consist in realising that the masters of the West couch their insight in terms of a way of spending time, a form of behaviour, whereas the Eastern texts speak directly about an inner attitude of mind. We therefore have to make a distinction between outward expression and the inner spirit informing any such expression. Then in the light of this distinction we can say that the East has seen more clearly what St Augustine and St Thomas have also seen but not stated so sharply, namely, that the essential thing is a certain attitude of mind, but that St Augustine and St Thomas have stated correctly that this attitude of mind does have priority and should be the object of our striving.

We can go on to say what this attitude of mind consists in. We seem to be in a position to say that in both West and East the essential thing in life from moment to moment is *neither* contemplation *nor* any particular activity as such but what can

12. at pp.125-126.

variously be called being devoted, dedicated, selfless, acting without being attached to the fruits of one's action, loving, doing the will of God, being abandoned to God, sacrificing oneself, cleaving to God, being joined to Him and therefore practising yoga in the etymological sense of being yoked – to the Origin and End of all things. At the same time we have to win through to such as inner attitude of mind and this is what detachment is about – which is therefore untilmately detachment from one's narrow possessive ego. So, to return to what you were saying, what the gradual overcoming of "cravings" and appetites is about is the detachment that liberates the one thing necessary, the inner state of mind that has been called devotion in the traditions of both West and East.'

'You have deepened and broadened what I was saying, Marcus, and as a result I can understand a little more clearly another passage from the *Bhagavad Gītā* which I wanted to bring out next, although I can now also see better just how much struggle is in fact involved in what is stated so simply, almost blandly:

> But the soul that moves in the world of senses and yet keeps the senses in harmony, free from attraction and aversion, finds rest in quietness.[13]

You see, even this classical spiritual text is not suggesting total abstinence. No, it states that it is possible for man to reach a state of purification such as to be able to surrender to his sensuality without being humiliated and pulled down by it.'

'I had overlooked that particular text, Martin, and yet I have lived for some time now with the more ancient text which I think must lie behind this one. It is the opening words of the *Iśā Upanishad*:

> All this, whatever moves on earth, is pervaded by the Lord. Renounce it first, and then enjoy.

13. II, 64, in the translation of Juan Mascaró.

This is the way in which Zaehner himself translates it, in his *Hinduism* again, but the real excitement of the message comes out when we realise that a subtly different translation can be given. This emerges from the fact that Gandhi translated it differently. Here is what Zaehner says:

> In his later years Gandhi was asked what he considered to be the essence of Hinduism, and he replied that the whole of Hinduism was contained in the first verse of the *Iśā Upanishad* which he translated as follows:
> All this that we see in this great universe is permeated by God.
> Renounce it and enjoy it.
> Do not covet anybody's wealth or possession.[14]

You see, the essential thing for me is that in Gandhi's rendering there is no mention of a before and after: *first* renounce, *then* enjoy. It's therefore as if in the concrete complexity of life either could come before the other, or they could even alternate indefinitely or be mingled with each other, so that the attitude which is being set before us as the goal of our seeking and struggle is an enjoyment *in* renunciation or a renunciation *in* the very enjoyment, a commitment which is nevertheless detached, a detachment which is nevertheless shot through with delight and laughter, a whole-hearted involvement with the world which is nevertheless so free as to amount to play. Is this perhaps what the Divine Comedy and the Hindu *lila*/game, *homo ludens*, man as playful and Śiva Nataraja, Lord of the Dance, are all about?'

'I think that you may have penetrated to the essence of what we're talking about, Marcus. I can, here, add only two further attempted formulations of the attitude of mind which a "serene way of life" is meant to bring about. The first is again from Steiner, in a passage where he is talking about the development of the state of consciousness called the six-petal lotus flower:

14. at p.180.

Still greater difficulty attends the development of the six-petalled lotus flower in the centre of the body, for it can be achieved only as the result of complete mastery of the whole man through consciousness of self, so that the body, soul and spirit are in perfect harmony. The functions of the body, the inclinations and passions of the soul, the thoughts and ideas of the spirit, must be turned to perfect unison. The body must be so ennobled and purified that its organs impel the individual to nothing that is not in the service of the soul and spirit. The soul must not be impelled, through the body, to desires and passions which conflict with pure and noble thinking. But the spirit must not dominate the soul with its laws and moral precepts like a slave-driver; the soul must follow these laws and duties out of its own free inclination. The pupil must not feel duty as a power hovering over him to which he unwillingly submits, but rather as something he does because he loves it. He must develop a free soul standing in equilibrium between sense, existence and spirituality. He must reach the stage where he may safely give himself over to his sense-nature, because this has been so purified that it has lost the power to drag him down to its level. It should no longer be necessary for him to curb his passions, because they will follow a right course of their own accord.[15]

The second passage contrasts strongly with it in tone, although not really in substance. Do you know Somerset Maugham's *The Razor's Edge*? It's about a young American, Larry, who is in search of illumination. He's an extremely entertaining character, liberated from the start and yet not a saint – an ascetic, if you like, but by nature and endowment and not by grace and struggle. He remains basically uninvolved although he is open, sociable, friendly. He is free even from sexual cravings, but because of his attractive tempera-

15. *Knowledge of the Higher Worlds*, at
    pp.137-138.

ment, he finds that women just crawl up to him, even into his bed, and he is kind enough to oblige. Here's the passage in which this state of mind is described by a woman who fell for him:

"I went upstairs and undressed and then slipped along the passage to his room. He was lying in bed reading and smoking a pipe. He put down his pipe and his book and moved to make room for me."

Suzanne was silent for a while and it went against my grain to ask her questions. But after a while she went on.

"He was a strange lover. Very sweet, affectionate and even tender, virile without being passionate, if you understand what I mean, and absolutely without vice. He loved like a hot-blooded schoolboy. It was rather funny and rather touching. When I left him I had the feeling that I should be grateful to him rather than he to me. As I closed the door I saw him take up his book and go on reading where he had left off."[16]

So here's a personality who's open, kind, free and completely untainted by the dark side of life and who acts out of a natural response to life.'

'That brings us down nice and easily from the heights we had ascended, Martin!

More seriously, I'd like to ask you a question which arises from all this. What you're here saying in effect is that we can have both a sexual and a contemplative life provided we fully recognise and appease the reality and insistence of sex in the context of a supporting way of life. Would you, therefore, say that there is in principle no conflict between sex and contemplation?'

'No, Marcus, I would not go as far as that. What I should say in this connection is two things. First, I now recall how many of the people I've dealt with and habitually move among, do practise meditation as an important part of their

16. at p.186.

lives but experience absolutely no conflict as a result. I was for a long time very puzzled by this, and I can only explain it by making a distinction between meditation and contemplation strictly so-called and saying that the meditation the people I have in mind practise, remains enclosed within the life they lead, whereas contemplation for me is a matter of gradually withdrawing from sensory and emotional stimuli, impressions and images and so disposing oneself to receive an influx of what St John of the Cross calls "the limpid light of God", being touched, in at least some measure, by pure spirit, and here one inevitably gets into conflict and struggle.'

'I see, so for you, meditation as you now speak of it tends to be a confirmation of the rest of life, whereas contemplation is a challenge to it, one is a sealing of ordinary life, the other is a breaking out of it, and this essentially because contemplation is an opening up to, a surrender to another, the Other, whose ways are not our ways? In other words, you would then, I think, endorse the searing words of the nineteenth century Russian master, Theophan the Recluse, recorded in that golden book about prayer, *The Art of Prayer*:

> God's grace, coming first at a man's initial awakening, and afterwards visiting him during the whole period of his conversion, cleaves him in two. It makes him aware of a duality within himself, and enables him to distinguish between what is unnatural and what should be natural; and thus it makes him resolve to sift or winnow all that is unnatural, so that his God-like nature should be brought fully to light. But obviously such a decision is only the beginning of the undertaking. At this stage it is only with his will and intention that he has left the domain of alien unnaturalness, rejecting it, and aiming at the naturalness which he expects and desires. But in fact his whole structure remains as before – that is saturated with sin; and passions dominate his soul in all its faculties and his body in all its functions, just as they did before – with only this difference, that formerly he chose and

embraced all this with desire and pleasure, but now, it is
not desired or chosen, but is hated, trampled on, rejected
...[17]

'Yes, I do strongly endorse this, and what you so aptly
quote brings me to the second thing I wanted to say in
response to your question about conflict between sex and
contemplation. You see, the goal of the contemplative pursuit
is indeed to be open to the influx of the "limpid light" but the
very effort has to pass via the tumult of emotional impulses,
facing the monsters of the deep, particularly but not exclusively sexuality, also anger, resentment, and so on; in fact it seems
to provoke them in a most daunting and terrifying way. St
John of the Cross is very clear and blunt about this:

Such, as we have said, is the night and purgation of sense
in the soul. In those who have afterwards to enter the
other and more formidable night of the spirit, in order to
pass to the Divine union of love of God (for not all pass
habitually thereto, but only the smallest number), it [the
way of illumionation or infused contemplation] is wont to
be accompanied by formidable trials and temptations of
sense, which last for a long time, albeit longer in some
than in others. For to some the angel of Satan presents
himself – namely, the spirit of fornication – that he may
buffet their senses with abominable and violent temptations, and trouble their spirits with vile considerations
and representations which are most visible to the
imagination, which things at times are a greater affliction
to them than death.[18]

William Johnston is entirely within this same tradition when
he writes as follows:

17. at p.140.
18. *The Dark Night of the Soul*, I,
   Chapter 14, at p.82.

When one begins to love profoundly at a new level of awareness (as often happens in deep intimacy between a man and woman) it may happen that latent or suppressed forces rise to the surface of the mind: hatred, jealousy, fear, insecurity, anger, suspicion, anxiety, unbridled eroticism and the rest surge up from the murky depths of the unconscious. And all this, it is well known, can coexist with true love. This violence, unleashed in human relations, can be unleashed also in the divine – the two are not so distinct, and divine love is incarnate. And one is liberated only by continuing to love. By fixing one's heart on the cloud of unknowing with deep peace, one becomes detached from these turbulent uprisings; and then they wither and die, leaving only love. It is by loving at the ultimate point, by going beyond all categories to the deepest centre, that one is liberated from jealousy and hatred and the rest. But this is an agonising purification.[19]

Just to indicate that once again we are dealing with something universally human, I'd like also to quote you another passage from Prabhavananda and Isherwood's commentary on Patanjali's *Yoga Sutras*:

When a spiritual aspirant begins to practice concentration, he meets all sorts of distractions. You never realise how much junk you have in the house until you start to clear out the attic and the cellar. You never realise how much rubbish has accumulated until you make the attempt to concentrate. Many beginners therefore become discouraged. "Before I started to practice concentration," they say, "my mind seemed fairly clean and calm. Now it's disturbed and full of dirty thoughts. It disgusts me. I'd no idea I was that bad! And surely I'm getting worse, not better?" They are wrong, of course. The very fact that they have undertaken a mental

19. *Silent Music*, at p.120.

house-cleaning, and stirred up all this mess, means that they have taken a step in the right direction. As for the calmness which they imagine they have hitherto experienced, it was nothing but apathy – the stillness of a pool which is choked with mud. To the casual observer, sloth and serenity – tamas and sattwa – may sometimes look alike. But to pass from the one to the other, we have to go through the violent disturbance of active effort – the phase of rajas. The casual observer, watching our struggles and our distress, may say: "He used to be much easier to get along with. I liked him better the way he was. Religion doesn't seem to agree with him." We must not mind that. We must continue our struggle, with all its temporary humiliations, until we reach that self-mastery, that one-pointedness of concentration, of which Paranjali speaks.[20]

'I see, Martin. So for you there's a scale and gradation of interests and activities, a process of moving from one stage to another, each of which must be respected and worked through before passing on to the next: the emotions must be satisfied and put in order, the sexual appetites must be appeased and humanised, meditation must be practiced and only then can we hope to become open to the contemplative experience. In fact this progression is strikingly reminiscent of the *Stufenfolge*, as you call it, the stairway, of movement from character training, through meditation and knowledge into the final liberation of the spirit in union which you expounded in chapter 5 of our previous series of conversations. It is that same stairway or scale but now with the specific inclusion of the sexual domain.

In this respect, however, I have a question. So far we have spoken about sex and contemplation as being in conflict and about sex reconciled with contemplation, but we have not spoken about whether sex can be said, in some way, to be

20. *How to Know God*, at pp.78-79.

taken up into the very essence of contemplation – the vexed subject of sublimation. We have moved, if you like, from sex *versus* contemplation, to sex *plus* contemplation, but we've not reached sex *into* contemplation. I could put this in terms of the famous vision of St Theresa, recorded in her autobiography and made the subject of a sculpture by Bernini:

> Our Lord was pleased that I should sometimes see a vision of this kind. Beside me, on the left hand, appeared an angel in bodily form, such as I am not in the habit of seeing except very rarely ... He was not tall but short, and very beautiful; and his face was so aflame that he appeared to me to be one of the highest rank of angels, who seem to be all on fire. They must be of the kind called cherubim, but they do not tell me their names. I know very well that there is a great difference between some angels and others, and between these and others still, but I could not possibly explain it. In his hands I saw a great golden spear, and at the iron tip there appeared to be a point of fire. This he plunged into my heart several times so that it penetrated to my entrails. When he pulled it out, I felt he took them with it, and left me utterly consumed by the great love of God. The pain was so severe that it made me utter several moans. The sweetness caused by this intense pain is so extreme that one cannot possibly wish it to cease, nor is one's soul then content with anything but God. This is not a physical, but a spiritual pain, though the body has some share in it – even a considerable share. So gentle is this wooing which takes place between God and the soul that if anyone thinks I am lying, I pray God, in His goodness, to grant him some experience of it.[21]

The really significant thing to my mind, for our present purposes, is that the mystical experience is couched in

21. *The Life of St Teresa*, translated by J.M. Cohen, at p.210.

explicitly sexual terms: the talk of wooing, the penetration of the phallic spear, the mixture of pain and delight, so that there is here an instinctive realisation on St Theresa's part of the truth that sexual powers are not pitted against contemplation but, on the contrary, are in their very essence taken up into the mystical experience. There is not conflict but transformation. Do you see?

'I do, and the question is very interesting. To take up your first point first, I should not only say that the scale, the gradation, the stairway of progress through sexual life into contemplation that I have evoked is the same as the stairway or scale which I had expounded before on the basis of the saying of the Buddha; I should go further and say that there is a sense in which the very act of love over a lifetime is inscribed with the same law of progression and is a foreshadowing of the act of contemplation.

You may remember that we identified four stages on the spiritual path: moral discipline, meditation, contemplation and union when the spirit becomes free. Now in making love we first learn to treat the other with consideration, feeling, tact – it will not do for the man, for instance, to come at the woman like a steamroller, as one woman once complained to me about her husband. This corresponds to the Buddha's stage of "character training" in life as a whole. Again in love-making we must not rush at the desired and loved object but need to approach gently, gradually probing, finding and penetrating; this corresponds to the Buddha's second stage of meditation, since this is a matter of approaching gently, weighing things, exploring, getting to know. The third correspondence is quite obvious because the chief word the Bible uses for sexual intercourse is knowing: He went into her and knew her. So this phase of intercourse, when we are sufficiently practised to find that we get to know each other in making love, corresponds to the Buddha's third stage of knowledge. Finally, the climax of love-making, the ecstasy, at least when there is a mutually achieved orgasm, corresponds to the Buddha's fourth stage of union. At the same time, I have to say that while the contemplative experience is forward-moving, developing and transforming, the sexual act, in my view, can be enjoyable and, for some couples, ideal, but it remains essentially repetitive. It is not the mystical way, only a shadow of it, a premonition of the life of the spirit.

I realise that I am left with the puzzle that it seems to be precisely those who experience sexual ecstasy who are so often not spiritual and not open to the spirit. I can only explain this to myself by thinking that the germ of such openness to the spirit is in all of us but that its flowering into the realm of the spirit depends on so many factors and accidents. This brings me to the importance of the counsellor but also to his limitations. For he can, by his awareness or lack of the dimension of the spirit within himself, facilitate or stunt the possible germination. At the same time it is not strictly his office directly and explicitly to waken this possibility, whereas it is that of the priest, as we have said before. So we have to recognise that the therapist strictly as therapist, by virtue of his training and outlook, does not go beyond psychic equilibrium and natural wisdom. It is up to the individual to realise that there is something beyond – stimulated, perhaps, by the priest.

Staying, however, with the counsellor, I do want to insist that he should be aware of this potentiality for the spirit in us all, and even of the extraordinary reach of this potentiality. This brings me to the main part of my response to your question. You asked whether there is a sense in which sex can turn *into* contemplation, whether the very sexual impulses and forces can be transformed into spiritual energy.

I have already suggested that it is precisely when a person begins to enter into the contemplative and mystical realm that sexual force gathers. It is as if these forces were threatened, and so mustered to resist, *but by this very token* became available to the victor.

At the same time the very absorption of sexual energies seems to be itself a matter of degrees. In this connection I have been very much struck by the difference of tone and language between, say, St Augustine, on the one hand, and St John of the Cross and St Theresa on the other. Take, for instance, this passage from St Augustine's *Confessions*:

> But what do I love when I love my God? Not material beauty or beauty of a temporal order; not the brilliance of earthly light, so welcome to our eyes; not the sweet melody of harmony and song; not the fragrance of flowers, perfumes, and spices; not manna or honey; not the limbs such as the body delights to embrace. It is not these that I love when I love my God. And yet, when I love Him, it is true that I love a light of a certain kind, a voice, a perfume, a food, an embrace; but they are of the kind that I love in my inner self, where my soul is bathed in light that is not bound by space; when it listens to sound that never dies away; when it breathes fragrance that is not borne away on the wind; when it tastes food that is never consumed by the eating; when it clings to an embrace from which it is not severed by fulfilment of desire. This is what I love when I love my God.[22]

It's very lovely, but it's still saturated with the memory of sensual experiences. Contrast this with St John of the Cross or St Theresa:

> Accordingly, a person should not mind if the operations of his faculties are being lost to him; he ought to desire rather that this be done quickly so that he may be no obstacle to the operation of the infused contemplation which God is bestowing, that he may receive it with more peaceful plenitude and make room in his spirit for the enkindling and burning of the love that this dark and secret contemplation bears and communicates to his soul. For contemplation is nothing else than a secret and

22. in the translation by R.S. Pine Coffin,
Penguin Classics, 1968, at pp.211-212.

peaceful and loving inflow of God, which, if not hampered, fires the soul in the spirit of love, as is brought out in the following verse:

Fired with love's urgent longings.[23]

So tranquilly and noiselessly does the Lord teach the soul in this state and do it good that I am reminded of the building of Solomon's temple, during which no noise could be heard; just so, in this temple of God, in this Mansion of His, He and the soul alone have fruition of each other in the deepest silence. There is no reason now for the understanding to stir, or to seek out anything, for the Lord who created the soul is now pleased to calm it and would have it look, as it were, through a little chink, at what is passing. Now and then it loses sight of it and is unable to see anything; but this is only for a brief time. The faculties, I think, are not lost here; it is merely that they do not work but seem to be dazed.'[24]

'So for you, Martin, the stairway or scale continues even in the contemplative realm itself? I find this very interesting. The essential idea, however, is that of this stairway or scale, of a progression of stages. What occurs to me, therefore, is that the way of life and human development which you envisage is strikingly like what has been incorporated into the very organisation of Hindu society. This is how K. M. Sen, a disciple of Rabindranath Tagore, puts it in his admirably simple account of Hinduism in the book of that name:

According to Hindu doctrines, the ideal life consists of four stages (āśramas): brahmacarya, the period of discipline and education, gārhasthya, the life of the householder and active worker, vānaprasthya, retreat for the loosening of bonds, and finally, sannyāsa, the life of a

23. *The Dark Night of the Soul*, I,
    Chapter 10, at p.318.
24. *Interior Castle*, VII, iii, at p.143.

hermit. *Brahmacarya* is an active period of education and hard work ... *Gārhasthya* is not looked upon as a less important period of life than the later ones, even though communication is such an important Hindu value. In a sense *gārhasthya* is considered to be the mainstay of the four *āśramas*, for it gives unity and cohesion to the entire structure, and the other *āśramas* depend on it for their sustenance. The Hindu is supposed to lead an active, married life at this stage, when ideals of social living are held to apply with particular force. It is often said that the Hindu ideal is inactivity, but in fact a considerable part of the Hindu scriptures discusses the value of an active life ... However, success in the wordly second period of life is not considered sufficient ... The successes of the material world, great as they are, are not considered sufficient, and it is here that the ideal of *moksha* or *mukti* comes in. This ideal of liberation is not a negative state. It is a state of completeness, of fullness of being, free from the bondage of *karma* and, thus, from rebirth ... The Hindu is supposed to loosen his association with the social life at the third stage, *vānaprasthya*, and later to lead the life of a hermit, *sannyāsa* ... Renunciation thus becomes an important part of ideal human life ...[25]

Now for me as a Roman Catholic, this extension of your own insight to become the principle of structuring the social life of the whole community is particularly fascinating. For, by means of this principle, the value of sexual renunciation is built into the very fabric of society as is it into the Roman Catholic regime of life, and yet this value is built into Hindu society in an importantly different way from the way this same value is built into the Roman Catholic community. In the difference lies the rub. For in the Roman Catholic way of seeking to honour and combine both values, sexual renunciation is recommended as an alternative to a sexual life for at

25. at pp.22-23.

least a few, where in the Hindu way it is seen as the culmination of sexual life for all. Moreover, in the Roman Catholic system, sexual renunciation is imposed as a way of life on all those who wish to be priests or religious even before they can be considered to have reached sexual maturity: sexual renunciation is a way of maturing in the Roman Catholic system and not only the fruit of maturing. I take it, however, Martin, from everything you've said that you would be totally opposed to this as going against human nature and its slowly ripening and developmental character? To be honest, to go back to where I started this morning, this is where the question of sex and contemplation becomes a daily anguish. This is why I find so much of what you say painful personally.'

'I, in my turn, found your opening, more personal remarks, almost too painful to bear myself. But, if you will allow me to say so, this really reinforces my point. I've already said that I value celibacy. I should go further and say that this truly noble ideal can be practised by a few. I think, for instance, again of my beloved St John of the Cross who certainly knew sexual temptations, as his very plain words show, but who had the gift of overcoming them and so manifesting to the rest of us a sublime ideal to which we need to strive in our own way. I think, personally, that his very bodily constitution – and for me it is relevant that he was physically a very small, short man – must have been of a particularly fine and delicately balanced character, so that he was not bothered and burdened by his body. But then he was also very spiritually centred. Be that as it may, I still think that this is for the very few and that we have to adapt the ideal to the vast majority precisely in order to make it accessible to them. All I can say is that in professional experience of priests, monks and nuns and those aspiring to the celibate life, I have witnessed such human misery, such chaos of perversions and substitutions, such ruin of the personal and even the religious life that I cannot speak strongly enough of the wrong-headedness of the system as an imposed system, regardless of individual human needs, wounds and weaknesses.'

'I recognise what you mean from my own professional experience, Martin, and yet I'm still bothered or borne up – I don't know which – by the thought that the Church cannot have been completely wrong for at least a thousand years to impose celibacy on aspiring priests, monks and nuns.'

'I agree, Marcus, you may be surprised to learn. For I have an immense regard for the wisdom of the Church and the sublime teaching of its greatest saints. But I'm talking about the Church as an establishment, which, as an establishment can perpetrate – and to my mind has perpetrated – untold and unnecessary unhappiness on so many people and in this area in particular.'

'Alright, Martin, limiting ourselves to the Church as an establishment, let me say that the nub of my difficulty about your statement when I'm squarely faced with it in terms of human development and happiness is that you talk as if a way of life – in our case a way of life which includes sexual renunciation – should be thought of only in terms of expressing something already possessed or gained, not a way of becoming what one can be, a form of practising what one wants to become. Yet surely there are certain important experiences in life which one can't prepare for adequately and which we therefore just have to embark on. We have to start doing them and learn in the doing. I mean, isn't, for example, marriage an experience in relationship which teaches one what one's capacity for reciprocal equality is about? In parenthood isn't it by being a parent that one practises what one is gradually able to become? As the French proverb well puts it, "C'est en forgeant qu'on devient forgeron", it's in doing the work of a smith that one becomes a smith. There are things in life, it seems to me, regimes, institutions, which are not realisations, expressions of what one already is but which are meant to be conducive to, bring out, what one can become. In the end they may become expressions of what one has become but they begin by being acts of trust and hope, means to becoming, ways of being initiated into what one wishes to be and can be. So, in a similar way, couldn't sexual renunciation be a way and a means towards, a practice of something one hopes to become and not just the expression of something already achieved? I find it interesting that some such view is to be found even within Hinduism. This is how M. Hiriyanna puts it in his excellent account of Hindu philosophy:

> The hexterodox held that man should once for all turn away from the world whatever his circumstances might be. But the orthodox regarded the ascetic ideal as only to be progressively realised ... The contrast between the two ideals is set forth in a striking manner in a chapter of the Mahābhārata known as the "Dialogue between Father and Son". Here the father, who represents the orthodox view, maintains that renunciation should come at the end of the āśrama discipline, but is won over to his side by the son, who holds the view that it is the height of unwisdom to follow amidst the many uncertainties of life such dilatory discipline and pleads for an immediate breaking away from all worldly ties.[26]

After all, you have yourself already stated that contemplation even within the context of a sexual life needs a "serene way of life" and that the purgative of work can include the spending of the vital and emotional energy of caring for and loving others. The practice of celibacy could therefore be seen as an extension of the "serene way of life" and as the cultivation of this work of caring.'

'I must say that I'm impressed by your counter-arguments, Marcus. At the very least they compel me to clarify certain things.

In the first place, I don't want to be taken to suggest that a sexual life – by which I mean a disciplined sexual life, above all in marriage – is a soft option. I can remember how shocked I was when I was having some analysis and the analyst said that marriage was the most difficult vocation. How green I must have been to be so surprised! Experience has taught me that

26. at pp.20-21.

sustained sexual life imposes its own requirements and that this is part of the necessary humanisation, let alone the spiritualisation of sex. It is indeed a training-ground for character and virtue in which inconsiderate habits gradually have to be weeded out and tolerance cultivated.

Secondly, I want to insist that when I say that everyone, in my opinion, has to pass through a sexual phase before aspiring to renounce sexual life, I don't necessarily mean a life-long sexual union. There are what I call *token* experiences. To take a fairly light-hearted example from my own experience, I can remember so vividly how, when I was fifteen year old, one of my uncles told me it was time to go with a prostitute and gave me the money – I can still see the very spot in the coffee house where he took me in hand. Well, I duly went to where the girls were parading and received their invitation, "Kommst du mit, Bubi?", "Are you coming, laddie?" but I found them so made up and odd, poor creatures, that I couldn't go further, and that was my experience of prostitutes for life. More seriously, what I have in mind is again something Steiner wrote in response to Friedrich Eckstein. He, you may know, was a very remarkable man, full of ancient wisdom, and he was to be seen holding court in the Kaffee Heinrichshof, opposite the Opera House, for half a lifetime. Steiner was told that Eckstein had decided that in order to experience life as a whole he would give himself up to unrestricted enjoyment. Steiner was appalled but, significantly, he waited to mature his response and then wrote as follows:

> The part of your letter which concerns Eckstein has shattered me. I have for a long time been aware that Friedrich Eckstein is in the grip of a fateful mistake. This consists of his understanding the sentence "A man must live his life through in all its fullness" in a wholly quantitative sense as if for him it were necessary to experience all the accidental and adventitious forms in which life's course manifests itself. This notion is mistaken in so far as it is tied to a misunderstanding

about the quality of all be..ig. For I too believe that the man of understanding must assume the substance of life and the world in all their forms into himself, but he must do this qualitatively, through deepening his experience more and more, and not through rushing around in all possible directions. This is not the way happiness lies since it leads to an infinite regress. The man of understanding must indeed live everything, but he must get his experience in the right places, not just wherever he happens to be pushed.[27]

You see, he was talking about a qualitative and not a quantitative testing of life.

All this said, however, I still maintain that celibacy is just not possible, except for the very few, and then as something freely chosen and grown towards as part of an individual self-determination. Personally I think that whatever may have been the situation before, people are no longer physically constituted the way they used to be. At the physical level alone, there are just more demands on the nerve centres of the brain. Take children. I've worked with children all my adult life and I have to say that they are now capable of grasping things – cars, computers, the new maths, the new astronomy – which leaves me feeling like a village idiot. But it's an established fact that the greater the intellectual work, whether academic work or, say, the work of a brain surgeon, the greater the nervous tension and also the sexual excitations, so that some relief is necessary. This is the sort of thing I have in mind when I talk of a change in people's constitution, the way they are incarnate and experience the balance of body and spirit.'

'Well, Martin, I must say that I still find myself torn between the evidence of so much human unhappiness caused by the attempt to impose celibacy on those unfitted for it and the intuition – instigated and reinforced by the Church – that

27. *Zu Rudolf Steiner's Lebensgang*, I,
     (1971), at p.136.

celibacy can be a valid part of a whole way of life and training as well as the fruit thereof. I realise, of course, that there's more to sex than celibacy. Yet the issue of celibacy focusses the issue of sexuality, making us concentrate on what sex is really about. I therefore do not regret our having included this issue in our present discussion, even at some length.

On this topic, you have, it seems to me, presented one side, on the basis of a coherent view of human development, while I have sought to present the other side, without anything like so convincingly an articulated a view to support that. Yet I feel that we have both shifted from our initial position and that we are groping towards some intermediate position which nevertheless still eludes us. I am tempted to say that this mediating position is to do with a view of human development and a regime of life which borrows something from, but lies beyond, the perceptions embodied in Hindu, the Roman Catholic and the Orthodox systems: the Hindu position that the sexual renunciation is the fruit of sexual life, the Roman Catholic position that sexual renunciation can be part of a whole way of maturing, and the Orthodox position that marriage is open even to priests but that celibacy is a condition for becoming a bishop. At the same time I also feel that this would still be grappling with the problem in too external a way. What we seem to need is some deepening and interiorising of the already current distinction between genital and general sexuality, and the perception – first just attained in its essence, then gradually embodied in appropriate structures – that the real choice and alternative is not between sexual life and sexual renunciation, but between *two modes of accepting and living ones' sexuality*. It may be that those who will show us this middle way will be not those dedicated either to marriage or virginity but those who feel such a lively attraction towards both counter-sexual friendship and God simultaneously that they have chosen the single state as another way of living their sexuality. It's just because such people are undistracted by the merely external rules and demands of either of the other two states that they can concentrate on the only thing that can sustain their constantly renewed choice, the inner substance of *both* marriage *and* consecrated virginity: the need for another human being in one state, the need for the source of selfhood in the other state, and the freedom *within* sexuality of both. It's this latter that seems to be the essential thing: freedom from the compulsive power of sexuality and therefore freedom in its regard, and in so far as we're talking about the freedom of getting beyond mere self-gratification, we seem to have come back to the idea of commerce with people and the world as *play*.

Be that as it may, for myself I must continue to struggle for my personal answer, conscious as I am in it that the celibacy I try to live is a discipline which could be changed so that my personal struggle may be part of a more general travail towards a different way of organising the balance between the two modes of living sexuality I've already indicated and towards a more subtle and humane way of discerning those who are psychologically capable of either state and those who are not.'

'With those last words of yours, Marcus, and especially with their very personal tone we seem to have come full circle. So I think that this is a suitable place at which to stop this morning. I should myself just like to say two last things.

First, before you had begun your final remarks I had myself already been thinking that there is more middle ground between us that may sometimes have appeared. And I was thinking in particular that we seemed to be agreed on two important things: that contemplation in some form must be an essential part of any fully human life, and that the prerequisite of any such contemplative life was what you called, by reference to St Thomas Aquinas, the need to be "quiet and calm". Where we differed was on the question whether it was possible to be "quiet and calm" without appeasing the sexual urge and attraction.

This is what I was beginning to formulate within myself. But having now heard your final remarks, I realise that what I really want to say by way of conclusion is to agree that the essence of what we've been talking about does still escape us, as you've said. At the same time, I think that our approaching the question of sexuality from opposite ends, as you said at the beginning, plus the further fact that we have indeed modified our initial views, have brought us a little closer to the heart of the matter. Perhaps that's the most we can hope for from our conversations: to focus on the live issues with as much purity of feeling and clarity of thought as we're capable of and then leave the working through to further discussions – and, above all, to life itself!'

'I'm quite happy to conclude at this point, Martin, as it were with a series of dots into the unknown ...'

Concluding Personal Postscript on Counselling and Friendship

Readers who have persevered so far will want to tie things together each in his or her own way. Any such gathering together of meanings and associations will be highly personal and I hope it will not intrude if I offer my own thoughts on re-reading what precedes. I want to foster such a process of recollection rather than distract from it.

My first thoughts, then, as I pondered the way our conversational explorations had gone, was to recur to one of the central themes of the book, namely, what it is to be human, and in particular to the fact that being human intrinsically involves a reference to a second, another. Being human is being one of at least two, becoming human requires the acknowledgement of another. I came back time and again to the late Professor John MacMurray's seminal intutition that 'the unit of the personal is not the "I" but the "you and I".'[1] Human-heartedness, as I found myself putting it, is an awareness of being half of two. We are insufficient to our sole selves. No man is an island, but a piece of the main. Anybody who has ever been in love implicitly knows this. One of the great poets of lyric love, E.E. Cummings has expressed his own variant of this discovery:

One's not half two. It's two are halves of one:
which halves reintegrating, shall occur
no death and any quantity.

1. *Persons in Relation* at p.61.

Finding one's other half is the first fulfilment of the pursuit and desire of the whole.

It is for this reason that dialogue is an enactment of what it is to be human. We engage in dialogue because we have a dialogical nature. Talking with another, ultimately playing with another, is exercising our human nature. Dialogue is the form of our human nature before it is a literary device, a more or less diverting if tricky option. Its appropriateness as a literary form derives from its ontological – my friend Dr Gregory would say its 'archetypal' – status.

In the light of this, however, the special characteristic and importance of counselling or psycho-therapy shine out with renewed clarity. For it is a dialogue and is as such the exercise of our dialogical nature. At the same time it is not a simple unimpeded dialogue but one that includes the impediments to an easier flow in its rationale. It is a conversation like any other but one that gathers the very difficulties into its own progress. It is like practising for full dialogue. It is to the extent that it thus pauses to work at the knots in relationship that it has a purpose and an authority of its own. It is concentrated. It is in principle free of such distractions as aimless chatter, mere gossip, ego-trips, even ego-trips *à deux*. This is how it is circumscribed, has its own boundaries, as the jargon has it. It is thus a conversation that takes place initially on the basis of various inequalities but that progressively comes to be on a more equally shared basis. In this sense it can be seen to be in the nature of an initiation into what it is to be more authentically human. We see better why *Gesprächstherapie*, talking therapy – at least when it is part and parcel of action-therapy, therefore indeed a 'form of life' – has privileged status. It is like art and theatre in relation to life: a mirror of life's deeper structures and patterns held up so as to return it to itself, more aware, more freely functioning, more compassionate.

The concentrated form of life that is therapy is thus meant to return us to ordinary life much as art does. But a distinction therefore remains between life in its privileged, intensified form and its daily, more diffuse form. At the same time our need for dialogue continues, in fact it is reinforced. So here a more piercing consequence of our dialogical being appears. To the extent that therapy successfully elicits the dialogical potential of any human being, it works with the capacity for relationship in us all but then it has to let the other pursue its completeness elsewhere, for the counsellor cannot *as such* be a friend in the ordinary sense of the word too – though he can become one once the specific task of therapy is concluded. The very experience of counselling or therapy can bring out capacities and raise expectations which cannot then be further fulfilled *in the therapy*.

By one of those strange coincidences that is, no doubt, not a coincidence, I learned this for myself in an acute way the very week I began writing this postscript. For it was during this time that I happened to be ending my own analysis after six years. I had felt at last that I had to cast off and yet I found it painful to do so – presumably because I had in the very experience of the relationship of analysis learned more deeply what relationship is, only then to realise that my analyst could not *qua* analyst reciprocate as an equal friend. The poignancy – and the chance – was that, for this, I had to look elsewhere.

So it tends to be in all therapy: the very contract and concentration points us beyond – in this case to the fulfilment of relationship that is friendship in its ordinary, daily sense.

For such friendship *is* the fulfilment we most deeply desire, isn't it? This is the logic of our being dialogical by nature, even more importantly it is the logic of our hearts: human-heartedness is the awareness of being half of two, and its natural name is friendship. In the light of this conclusion of head and heart alike, therapy and counselling themselves take on a different look. There are different theories as to what therapy is about – listening, catalysing, holding, transference, companioning, and so on – but these theories rise and fall, mercifully so, since the reality of relationship is more complex and mysterious than is dreamt of in any philosophy. So can we not say, both more simply and more complexly, that therapy is not this element or that, but all of them? It is not, say, holding, but then neither is it, say, withholding, nor empathy, acceptance or congruence, exploring or waiting, confronting, befriending, accompanying, attending, enjoying. It is not any one of these alone, it is all of them. But we can now see that it is also all these as rehearsals and adumbrations of the flow of friendship in all *its* moments and positions. For in the growth and gradual deployment of human relationship there is feeding and playing, suckling and rearing, taking in and giving out, incorporation and evacuation, withholding and releasing, touching base and exploration, the rhythm of withdrawal and return, going in and coming out, in and out, coupling and uncoupling, the various making and loosing of affectional bonds, whatever, what have you. All these can be seen as so many trailers and variants of the central mystery of the self and other – the play and interplay of my mother, my self, me and you; the struggle between pride and oppression, omnipotence and impotence, self-sufficiency and dependence, the sin of Lucifer and the solidarity of love; the aspiration to union without fusion, as all this receives its consummation in friendship – sexual friendship usually, and yet not only.

For there is a still further pointer beyond. This thought too emerged for me as I re-read our dialogues. In the third dialogue my friend Dr Gregory was talking most movingly about certain meetings which operate primarily through gazing and which have about them an air of being predestined. As I re-read this, I thought again of John Donne's poem 'The Good Morrow'. He began by asking, much as the lovers Dr Gregory mentioned might have done:

I wonder by my troth, what thou, and I
Did, till we lov'd? Were we not wean'd till then?

Then at the end of the first stanza he answers:

If ever any beauty I did see,
Which I desir'd, and got, t'was but a dreame of thee.

This is a metaphysical enough sentiment as it is, but suppose we were to take the essential insight and transpose it onto an even higher metaphysical plane? The poet perceives that any previous loves are but an anticipation of the definitive love between two human beings. Can we not prolong this thought and say that the delicate, intimate and seemingly predestined sort of human meeting that sometimes occurs is itself only an anticipation and foreshadowing of the final face-to-face with God?

If this is so, then certain other things also fall into place. The reason of the heart even more than reason itself is to realise the need of a dialogical other, to find the peer and companion of one's heart, to be able to say with another contemporary poet, Elizabeth Jennings 'I felt myself, acknowledged you', and yet to realise that even with such friendship the heart is restless until it rests in God. Not that it is a matter of a friend *or* God. No, most vehemently no. Just as therapy can prepare for ordinary friendship and friendship in turn for God, so God's most urgent desire and work is to make us more and more fully human and therefore more and more capable of exercising human relationship in all its forms. It is man fully alive and human that is the glory of God; grace perfects nature, and grace, as St Thomas Aquinas saw, is a *law* which precisely as such integrates man into society, makes him social, associated, so that morality is being patient of progressively but creatively assuming the mores of one's tribe and people and, finally, the human race. The effect of therapy should therefore be to promote the growth into that being human and so being more and more generously related which culminates in being God's steward and his spy, as King Lear puts it; his eye, his veritable exemplification and image. But correspondingly the effect of any spirituality we may be granted is to centre us in our most radical relationship so that it can flower into human relationships. Here there is in principle no more split than there is between inner and outer, centre and radii, root and flower, *physis*/nature and metaphysics.

That's perhaps the rub for some. This *is* being very metaphysical, not to say solemn. Yet even such glimmerings suggest another light and horizon, as does human dialogue at its most intimate and pure. For a truly human dialogue of head and heart tends towards play, *krida*. But that is another story, for another time ...

Index of Works Cited

Aquinas, Thomas *Summa Theologica*
Augustine *Confessions*
Augustine *The City of God*

Baden, H.J. *Wissende, Verschwiegene, Eingeweihte* (Herder, Munich, 1981)
Bancroft, A. *Twentieth Century Mystics and Sages* (William Heinemann, London, 1976)
Bhagavad Gītā
Brown, D. & Pedder, J. *Introduction to Psychotherapy* (Tavistock Publications, London, 1979)

Igumen Chariton of Valamo *The Art of Prayer* (Faber & Faber, London, 1966)

Fiedler, L. *Max Reinhardt* (Rowohlt Taschenbuch Verlag, Reinbek bei Hamburg, 1975)
Finnis, J. *Natural Law and Natural Rights* (Oxford University Press, Oxford, 1980)
Fromm, E. *The Art of Loving* (George Allen & Unwin, London, 1975)
Furlong, M. *Travelling In* (Hodder & Stoughton, London, 1971)

Gadamer, H.G. *Truth and Method* (Sheed & Ward, London, 1975)
Goethe *Faust*
Goethe *Iphigenie auf Tauris*
Green, T.H. *Prologomena to Ethics* (Oxford University Press, Oxford, 4th edition, 1899)
Gregory, Pope *Moralia in Job*

Harding, E. *The Way of All Women* (Rider & Co., London, 1971)

Heyer, C.G. *Der Organismus der Seele* (Ernst Reinhardt Verlag, Munich, 1951)

Hiriyanna, M. *Outlines of Indian Philosophy* (George Allen & Unwin, London, 1932)

Jacobi, J. *A Jung Anthology* (Pantheon Books, New York, 1953)

James, W. *Varieties of Religious Experience* (Longman, Green & Co., London, 1910)

John of the Cross, *The Dark Night of the Soul* (Burns & Oates, London, 1953)

Johnston, W. *Silent Music* (William Collins Sons & Co., Glasgow, 1974)

Klein, M. *Our Adult World and its Roots in Infancy* (Tavistock Publications, London, 1960)

Laing, R.D. *The Divided Self* (Penguin Books, Harmondsworth, Middx, 1965)

MacMurray, J. *Persons in Relation* (Faber & Faber, London, 1961)

MacVicar, R. *Healing Through Meditation* (Scottish Centre of Christian Healing, Boness, n.d.)

Mandel, S. *Rainer Maria Rilke* (Southern Illinois University Press, 1965)

Maugham, S. *The Razor's Edge* (Penguin Books, Harmondsworth, Middx, 1963)

Merton, T. *Conjectures of a Guilty Bystander* (Doubleday Books, New York, 1968)

Morgenstern, C. *Epigramme und Sprüche* (Piper Verlag, Munich, 1922)

Newman, J.H. *An Essay of the Development of Christian Doctrine* (Penguin Books, Harmondsworth, Middx, 1974)

Paul, *Epistle to the Colossians*

Prabhavananda & Isherwood, C. *How to Know God – The Yoga Aphorisms of Patanjali* (Vedanta Press, Hollywood, 1966)

Reiter, U. *Meditation: Wege zum Selbst* (Mosaik Verlag, Munich, 1976)

Rilke, R.M. *Briefe an einen Jungen Dichter* (Insel Bücherei, Band 406, n.d.)

Rilke, R.M. *Winterliche Stanzen* (Insel Verlag, Leipzig, 1957)

Rittelmeier, F. *Die Christengemeinschaft* (Letzte Predigt, 1938)

Rogers, C. *On Becoming a Person* (Constable & Co, London, 1967)

Rosenberg, A. *Die Zauberflöte* (Prestel Verlag, Munich, 1972)

Sandler, J., Dare, C. & Holder, A. *The Patient and the Analyst* (Maresfield Reprints, London, 1982)

Sen, K.M. *Hinduism* (Penguin Books, Harmondsworth, Middx, 1981)

Shakespeare, W. *Henry V*

Shakespeare, W. *Macbeth*

Shakespeare, W. *The Tempest*

Silva, J. & Miele, P. *The Silva Method of Mind Control* (Grenada Publishing, Herts, 1980)

Steiner, R. *Die Welt der Sinne und die Welt des Geistes* (Rudolf Steiner Verlag, Dornoch bei Basel, Switzerland, 1959)

Steiner, R. *Knowledge of the Higher Worlds* (Rudolf Steiner Press, London, 1969)

Steiner, R. *Zu Rudolf Steiners Lebensgang*, Bildband I (Verlag Die Kommenden, Freiburg im Breisgau, 1971)

Swailes, M. *Arthur Schnitzler* (Oxford University Press, London, 1971)

Theresa of Avila *The Life of Saint Teresa* (Penguin Books, Harmondsworth, Middx, 1958)

Theresa of Avila *Interior Castle* (Sheed & Ward, London, 1974)

Weigand, H.J. ed. *Goethe, Wisdom and Experience* (Routledge & Kegan Paul, London, 1949)

White, V. *How to Study* (Aquin Press, London, 1966)

Williams, H. *The True Wilderness* (Fontana & Collins, Glasgow, 1965)

Wilson, C. *New Pathways in Psychology: Maslow and the Post-Freudians* (Victor Gollancz, London, 1973)

Winnicott, D. *Playing and Reality* (Penguin Books, Harmondsworth, Middx, 1982)

Wordsworth, W. *Lines Composed a Few Miles above Tintern Abbey*

Zaehner, R.C. *Hindu Scriptures* (J.M. Dent & Sons, London, 1972)

Zaehner, R.C. *Hinduism* (Oxford University Press, Oxford, 1980)